CAMBRIDGE IBERIAN AND LATIN AMERICAN STUDIES

GENERAL EDITOR
P. E. RUSSELL F.B.A.
Emeritus Professor of Spanish Studies
University of Oxford

ASSOCIATE EDITORS
E. PUPO-WALKER
Director, Center for Latin American and Iberian Studies
Vanderbilt University
A. R. D. PAGDEN
Lecturer in History, University of Cambridge

Tragicomedy and Novelistic Discourse
in *Celestina*

The late fifteenth-century Spanish masterpiece *Celestina* is one of the world's most neglected classics. In this important study one of the most recent editors of the text, Dorothy Sherman Severin, investigates how Fernando de Rojas' work in dialogue, which parodies earlier genres, is a precursor of the modern novel.

In *Celestina*, the hero Calisto parodies the courtly lover, the heroine Melibea lives through classical examples and popular song, Calisto's servants Sempronio and Parmeno parody students' knowledge, the bawd and go-between Celestina deals a blow to the world of wisdom literature, and Melibea's father Pleberio gives his own gloss on the lament. There is also a fatal clash between two literary worlds, that of the self-styled courtly lover (the fool) and the prototype picaresque world of the Spanish Bawd and her mentors (the rogues). The voices of *Celestina* are parodic, satiric, ironic and occasionally tragic, and it is in their discourse that the dialogic world of the modern novel is born.

In order to make this book accessible to a wider English-speaking readership, quotations from the text are accompanied by English translations, mainly from the seventeenth-century English version by James Mabbe.

T0370591

Celestina knocks on Melibea's door while Melibea and Lucrecia are in the garden awaiting the arrival of Calisto and his servants; Calisto and Elicia chat with Sempronio and Pármeno in the foreground.

Tragicomedy and Novelistic Discourse in *Celestina*

DOROTHY SHERMAN SEVERIN

University of Liverpool

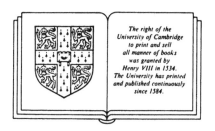

The right of the
University of Cambridge
to print and sell
all manner of books
was granted by
Henry VIII in 1534.
The University has printed
and published continuously
since 1584.

CAMBRIDGE UNIVERSITY PRESS

CAMBRIDGE

NEW YORK   NEW ROCHELLE

MELBOURNE   SYDNEY

CAMBRIDGE UNIVERSITY PRESS
Cambridge, New York, Melbourne, Madrid, Cape Town, Singapore,
São Paulo, Delhi, Dubai, Tokyo

Cambridge University Press
The Edinburgh Building, Cambridge CB2 8RU, UK

Published in the United States of America by Cambridge University Press, New York

www.cambridge.org
Information on this title: www.cambridge.org/9780521122832

First published 1989
This digitally printed version 2009

A catalogue record for this publication is available from the British Library

Library of Congress Cataloguing in Publication data
Severin, Dorothy Sherman.
Tragicomedy and novelistic discourse in Celestina / Dorothy
Sherman Severin
p.   cm. – (Cambridge Iberian and Latin American studies)
Bibliography.
Includes index.
ISBN 0-521-35085-9
1. Rojas, Fernando de, d. 1541. Celestina. 2. Rojas, Fernando
de, d. 1541. Celestina – Sources. 3. Wit and humor in literature.
I. Title. II. Series.
PQ6428.S44   1989
862'.2 – dc19   89-496 CIP

ISBN 978-0-521-35085-3 Hardback
ISBN 978-0-521-12283-2 Paperback

Contents

Illustrations

Preface

If some of the chapters of this monograph look strangely familiar, it is because, during a long gestation period, they have appeared, usually in a different form, or have been delivered orally and occasionally published in the *actas* of a learned conference. Textual antecedents and first drafts of some of the chapters in this book can be found in the bibliography. It was my original intention to concentrate on humour in *Celestina*, but the topic took some unexpected turns, and the relationship of *Celestina* with its sources – what we now, unfortunately, call intertextuality – became a prime consideration, along with the question of genre in its most recent manifestation as 'novelistic discourse'.

I am indebted to my former Westfield colleague and dear friend Alan Deyermond, who has seen (or heard) much of this material and commented on it. My mentor Stephen Gilman, who disagreed with my conclusions about genre and *Celestina* but gamely agreed to look at them and discuss them with me, died before this little book went to press, and I would like it to dedicate to his memory. Without his teaching and influence I would never have come to *Celestina* studies.

Dorothy Sherman Severin
Liverpool

Abbreviations

BHS   *Bulletin of Hispanic Studies*
Ce.   *Celestinesca*
Clas. Cast.   *Clásicos Castellanos*
CSIC   Consejo Superior de Investigaciones Científicas
CUP   Cambridge University Press
EUDEBA   Editorial Universitario de Buenos Aires
HR   *Hispanic Review*
KRQ   *Kentucky Romance Quarterly*
LCL   Loeb Classical Library
Neophil.   *Neophilologus*
NRFH   *Nueva Revista de Filología Hispánica*
OUP   Oxford University Press
PSA   *Papeles de Son Armadans*
RF   *Romanische Forschungen*
RFE   *Revista de Filología Española*
RoN   *Romance Notes*
RPh   *Romance Philology*
TWAS   Twayne's World Authors Series
UNCSRLL   University of North Carolina Studies in Romance Languages and Literatures

Calisto and Melibea's first encounter in the garden. Calisto's falcon is
perched in a tree.

I

Introduction: *Celestina* and novelistic discourse

The characters of *Celestina* essentially occupy inner space, rather than living outdoors in linear space.[1] The scenes of *Celestina* take place in people's houses and gardens and not on the open road, in contrast with the chivalric romance, or the later picaresque genre, or *Don Quixote*, where interiors exist but are not the rule. This may be explained by *Celestina*'s genesis in the humanistic comedy and the sentimental romance. Arnalte's 'triste morada' [sad dwelling] in the *Tratado de amores de Arnalte y Lucenda*, or Leriano's jail of love in *Cárcel de Amor*, prefigure *Celestina*, although the later book's houses are only incidentally allegorical or symbolic. *Celestina* shows in its use of inner space a curious parallel with the nineteenth-century novel which occurs indoors, though we might equally cite the initial requirements of stagecraft (the humanistic comedy which influences the author of Act I) as predisposing the book to interiors. Celestina's brothel and laboratory, Pleberio's mansion and Melibea's garden, Calisto's house and stable, are the background against which the voices of *Celestina* meet and speak. The anti-heroic Celestina herself is seen sallying forth on the open road, occasionally with her picaresque Sancho, Sempronio, but she leaves her own house to proceed to Melibea's and then back again, or to Calisto's to report her success. Pármeno and Calisto also travel to and from their assignations with their respective women, but the boudoir or garden is their goal.

As I shall show in this monograph, the voices of *Celestina* are parodic, satiric, ironic, and occasionally tragic, and it is in their discourse, which Bakhtin calls, rather obscurely, double-voiced and internally dialogized discourse, that the dialogic world of the modern novel is created:[2]

The fundamental condition, that which makes a novel a novel, that which is responsible for its stylistic uniqueness, is the speaking person and his discourse. (332)

Examples of this would be comic, ironic or parodic discourse, the refracting discourse of a narrator, refracting discourse in the language of a character, and finally the discourse of a whole incorporated genre. (324)

Looking briefly at our dramatis personae, we will see that Calisto parodies the courtly lover, Melibea lives through classical example and popular song, Sempronio and Pármeno parody students' lore and knowledge,[3] Celestina deals a blow to the world of aphorism and wisdom literature, and even Pleberio gives his own gloss on the lament. We also have a fatal clash of two literary worlds, that of the self-styled courtly lover (the fool) and the prototype picaresque world of the Spanish Bawd and her minions (the rogues).

Celestina is a generic hybrid: neither humanistic comedy nor sentimental romance, it creates its own new dialogic and novelistic genre which prefigures the world of both *Lazarillo* and *Don Quixote*. The narrator, omniscient or otherwise, is not, it is true, present in *Celestina*; but the narrator is not an essential ingredient of the novel. For Bakhtin, it is dialogue which defines the genre: 'Thus even where . . . there is no narrator, no posited author or narrating character, speech diversity and language stratification still serve as the basis for style in the novel' (315).

Bakhtin's distinction between what he calls 'First Stylistic Line' and 'Second Stylistic Line' novels can also be helpful to us here: for our purposes the chivalric romances represent the First Line, while *Lazarillo* and *Don Quixote* represent the Second Line.

> Novels of the Second Stylistic Line, transform this already organized and ennobled everyday and literary language [from First Line Novels] into essential material for its own orchestration, and into people for whom this language is appropriate, that is, into 'literary' people with their literary way of thinking and their literary ways of doing things – that is, such a novel transforms them into authentic characters. (383)

Furthermore we have the testing-of-the-hero device which Bakhtin claims is characteristic of the early novel in particular:

> Already in *Don Quixote* we have a literary, novelistic discourse being tested by life, by reality. And in its further developments, the novel of the Second Line remains in large measure a novel that tests literary discourse [and] concentrates the critique and trial of literary discourse around the hero – a 'literary man' who looks at life through the eyes of literature and who tries to live according to literature. (412)

Although *Celestina* is not centred on a single hero or anti-hero but several, a full century before *Don Quixote* we have in *Celestina* characters who try to live life through literature; for one, courtly literature, for another, classical literature and ballads, for a third, aphoristic literature. What we lack is the playful persona of the narrator pretending not to be the narrator, who enters the novelistic world as an intermediary between the alleged author, Cide Hamete, and the reader: the non-omniscient narrator, living from instalment to instalment. Instead we have the absent narrator, Rojas, who hides in a letter and a prologue, then behind Petrarch, then behind the voices of his characters, and finally behind acrostics. The voices of *Celestina* are human beings in metamorphosis, as Lazarillo will be nearly half a century later. Even the cardboard Calisto finally emerges as the hero of imagination.[4] The transformations of Melibea and Pármeno (our pseudo-Aristotelian scholar), have been studied by Gilman in his seminal masterpiece, *The Art of 'La Celestina'*. Although Celestina develops least of the characters, since she is already at the end of the road of her life, her memories hint at a lifetime of metamorphosis and mutability, as I tried to show in *Memory in 'La Celestina'*. The prostitutes (who seem to have been admirers of the Archpriest of Talavera's female creations) change so dramatically that María Rosa Lida de Malkiel claimed that they swap characters between the *Comedia* and the *Tragicomedia*.[5] And Pleberio's sheltered edifice against Fortuna's vicissitudes (and undoubtedly he was trying to live through Boethius and Petrarch) lies in ruins at the end of the work.

Jerry Rank, in a recent article,[6] has written of narrativity in *Celestina*, relating it to ideas proposed by Genette and Barthes, and developing the notion of narrativity in memory which I first proposed in *Memory in 'La Celestina'*:

> In conclusion, I do not claim that *La Celestina* represents a developed novelistic narrative style, but that there does seem to be a process peculiar to later narrative forms embedded in its text, which sporadically surfaces. It is . . . triggered by preoccupation with a past which infringes on the dialogic present of the work and stretches the frame to include it. It is a process which blends the present with the past and establishes a personal narrative by complexity and depth. (245)

Finally, I would also like to invoke the aid of Alastair Fowler and his landmark contribution to generic theory, *Kinds of Literature: an Introduction to the Theory of Genres and Modes*.[7] He points out, not only that 'when we try to decide the genres of a work, then, our aim is to discover its meaning'

(38), but even more essentially that 'Every literary work changes the genres it relates to . . . Consequently all genres are continuously undergoing metamorphosis. This, indeed, is the principal way in which literature itself changes' (23). In this monograph I will try to demonstrate that *Celestina*, despite the absence of a third-person narrator, is the first work in world literature which can qualify for the title 'novel' rather than 'romance'. I agree with Edwin Williamson that of the other possible contenders, neither *Orlando Furioso* nor *Tirant lo Blanc* is a novel despite parodic elements:

For all their misgivings about the idealized world of chivalry, Ariosto and Martorell are ultimately trapped by genre: the conventions of romance determine the structure of their narratives and shape the experience of their characters. In the *Quixote*, however, the entire world of chivalric romance exists nowhere other than inside the mad hero's head. (81)[8]

I develop my arguments first through an examination of the author's own statements in the prologues, the prologue poetry and the epilogue poetry ('the intentional fallacy' as it is now called). I then move on to an examination of courtly parody, of the uses of satire, and of the movement in the work from comedy to tragedy. Rojas' uses of other genres, generic experimentations, and distortions of genre will be paramount in these considerations. By challenging and redefining previous genres, Rojas forges a new generic hybrid which becomes the first modern novel.

This conclusion may seem merely to be a return to the position adopted by Menéndez y Pelayo when he discussed *Celestina* in his *Orígenes de la novela*,[9] although he insisted on the novel's dramatic qualities as well and called it a precursor of both novel and drama in Spain. He also studied *Celestina*'s dramatic antecedents, particularly the Italian humanistic comedy in Latin, an approach adopted by María Rosa Lida de Malkiel as well in *La originalidad artística de 'La Celestina'.*[10] Although I agree with her that whereas the first authors set out to write a humanistic comedy, as Alan Deyermond[11] has pointed out, Rojas seems rather to have moved in the direction of the tragic sentimental romance when he took up the pen of his predecessor. But it is not just length or new seriousness of purpose which leads me to my conclusion, but the examination of Rojas' critical attitudes to his sources and his parodic, satiric and ironic treatment of them which leads him to forge a new genre.

One final word about the authorship problem before we move on to a closer reading of the text of *Celestina*. Miguel Marciales in his newly published edition of *Celestina*[12] has made some startling suggestions about the authorship of the work: that the original author must have been Rodrigo Cota, and that the additional *Tragicomedia* acts x, xv, xvii and xviii (the 'Tratado de Centurio') were not written by Rojas but possibly by Sanabria, the author of the 'Auto de Traso' (xviiib), which appears in some late editions of the *Celestina*. I have tried to refute these arguments elsewhere[13] and shall not rehearse my opinions again here, other than to say that I will still refer to the author of Act i as an anonymous 'primitive' author, and that I still accept Rojas' authorship of the 'Tratado de Centurio', despite agreeing with Marciales that Act xviii in particular is rather inferior to Rojas' usual standards. María Rosa Lida de Malkiel may have been closer to the mark when she postulated some sort of group composition – Rojas with the help of his friends – at least for the 'Tratado de Centurio'.

2

The prefatory material: the author's ambivalent intentions

Pármeno opens the door to let Sempronio and Celestina into Calisto's house.

2

The prefatory material: the author's ambivalent intentions

The comic aspect of *Celestina* has been given short shrift in twentieth-century criticism.[1] Its ironies have been studied, but principally its tragic ironies and not its comic ones.[2] The relation of the work to its classical and Italian humorous antecedents has also been scrutinized, but mainly from the perspective of literary sources.[3] Only parody has been studied from the humorous angle.[4] Yet Rojas himself tells us that he began his work by finding a funny book. He decided to continue it in the same vein, although his own tragic ending altered the character of the work enough to force him to change the title into a hybrid form so that the *Comedia de Calisto y Melibea* became the *Tragicomedia* in its expanded version:

Otros han litigado sobre el nombre, diciendo que no se había de llamar comedia, pues acababa en tristeza, sino que se llamase tragedia. El primer autor quiso darle denominación del principio, que fue placer, y llamóla comedia. Yo viendo estas discordias, entre estos extremos partí agora por medio la porfia, y llaméla tragicomedia.[5] (43)

[Others have contended about the name, saying that it ought not to be called a comedy, because it ends in sorrow and mourning, but rather termed it a tragedy. The author himself would have it take its denomination from its beginning, which treats of pleasure, and therefore called it a comedy. So that I, seeing these differences,

9

between their extremes have parted this quarrel by dividing it in the midst, and call it a tragi-comedy.]

In fact, there is little that is inheréntly more tragic in the additional acts, which are by their nature primarily comic. Thus Rojas' friends, he tells us, were quibbling about the nature of the original *Comedia*. Some of them called it a tragedy but Rojas disagreed and renamed it a tragicomedy. Nor was he the first author to have this problem of terminology. When Plautus wrote his comic *Amphitryon* about the gods, he admitted that because it concerned the gods it should be called a tragedy, and so he would have to compromise, just as Mercury tells us in the Prologue: 'I shall mix things up: Let it be tragicomedy.'[6] One might point out that for Rojas 'comedy' implied not only dialogue form but comic content as well. And Plautus had supplied him with a useful tag, tragicomedy, perhaps (as F. Castro Guisasola suggests) via Verardo's *Fernandus Servatus*,[7] although Plautus' problem was entirely different from Rojas' one. Plautus had a comedy which dealt with serious figures; Rojas had a comic work with a tragic ending.

Besides correcting those readers who wanted to designate the work a tragedy, on numerous occasions in his prefatory material Rojas reiterates the fact that there is a comic and even lewd side to the work, using the 'sugared pill' metaphor so popular in didactic literature of the period. He is careful to point out the humour in the work and to warn the reader not to be totally distracted by it from his more serious purpose. Thus in the letter from the author to a friend which appeared in the original sixteen-act *Comedia*, he praises Act i for its humour and its serious purpose alike:

Vi, no sólo ser dulce en su principal historia o ficción toda junta, pero aun de algunas de sus particularidades salían deleitables fontecicas de filosofía, de otros agradables donaires, de otros avisos y consejos contra lisonjeros y malos sirvientes y falsas mujeres hechiceras. (36)

[I saw that it was not just sweet in its main story or fiction as a whole, but even that from some of its details delightful founts of philosophy emanated, from others agreeable jokes, from others advice and counsel against flattering and evil servants and false witches (my translation).]

The original author is worthy of praise: 'es digno de recordable memoria por la sotil invención, por la gran copia de sentencias entrejeridas, que so color de donaires tiene' [it is worthy of memorable note on account of the subtle invention, the great quantity of *sententiae* which are interwoven disguised as pleasantries (my translation)].

He reiterates this verdict in his prefatory poem in the *Comedia*: 'Vi que portaba sentencias dos mil / en forro de gracias, labor de placer' (39). [I saw that it had two thousand *sententiae* / a work of pleasure lined with pleasantries (my translation).] As for his own contribution, it is the sugar on the bitter pill: 'De esta manera mi pluma se embarga, /imponiendo dichos lascivos, rientes, / atrae los oídos de penadas gentes' (38). [In this way my embarassed pen, /writing sayings which are lascivious, joking, / attracts the ears of suffering people (my translation).] He gives a clue to the meaning of the work in these verses:

Si bien discernéis mi limpio motivo,
a cuál se endereza de aquestos extremos,
con cuál participa, quién rige sus remos,
amor apacible o desamor esquivo,
buscad bien el fin de aquesto que escribo,
o del principio leed su argumento:
leeldo y veréis que, aunque dulce cuento,
amantes, que os muestra salir de cativo. (st. 4, 38)

[If you indeed wish to discern my clean motive,
or what I aim at from these extremes,

or who pilots it, who guides its oars –
peaceable love or scornful dislike –
look at the end of what I am writing;
or read the argument at the beginning,
read it and you will see that although a sweet story,
lovers, it shows you how to escape from captivity
(my translation).]

The purpose of the *Comedia*, according to Rojas, is to show lovers how to escape from the captivity of love, and he recommends that we look at the *argumento de toda la obra* [summary of the whole work] and at Pleberio's lament ('el fin de aquesto que escribo'). This stanza is corroborated by his introduction to his friend and patron: not only does the country need *Celestina*, but so does this friend, 'cuya juventud de amor ser presa se me representa haber visto y de él cruelmente lastimada, a causa de le faltar defensivas armas para resistir sus fuegos' (36) [whose youth I recall having seen a captive to love and cruelly tormented by it, because of your lack of defensive arms to resist its fires (my translation)].

Unfortunately Rojas' stated purpose in the *Comedia* has been confused with the opinions of his first editors, who undoubtedly wrote the moralistic *incipit* as well as the individual *argumentos* [summaries] of the sixteen acts,[8] and Rojas tells us in his new prologue ('Que aún los impresores han dado sus punturas, poniendo rúbricas o sumarios al principio de cada auto' 43) [The printers, they likewise have bestowed their puncture, putting titles, and adding Arguments to the beginning of every act . . .]. According to his editors, the work was composed

en reprehensión de los locos enamorados, que, vencidos en su desordenado apetito, a sus amigas llaman y dizen ser su dios. Asimismo hecho en aviso de los engaños de las alcahuetas y malos y lisonjeros sirvientes (44)

[in reprehension of those foolish and brain-sick lovers who, over-
come by their disordinate appetites, cleep their lovers their gods; as
also made for our advice and admonition; wherein we are warned
to take heed of the deceits and subtleties of bawds, of the craftiness
of false and flattering servants].

In the *Tragicomedia* there is a marked change of emphasis
in Rojas' tone, and he has added a final stanza to the
introductory verses:

O damas, matronas, mancebos, casados,
notad bien la vida que aquéstos hicieron,
tened por espejo su fin cuál hobieron;
a otro que amores dad vuestros cuidados.
Limpiad ya los ojos, los ciegos, errados,
virtudes sembrando con casto vivir,
a todo correr debéis de huir,
no os lance Cupido sus tiros dorados. (st. 11, 40)

[O ladies, matrons, youths, spouses,
note well the life that these led,
take the ending they met as a mirror;
give your attention to something beside love,
wipe your eyes, blind and lost,
sow virtues with chaste lives;
you should flee with all speed,
let not Cupid shoot his gilded arrows at you (my translation).]

This is far more didactic in tone than the original stanza
which it replaces, a general contemplation of the Crucifixion
and a generalized exhortation to virtue:

Olvidemos los vicios que así nos prendieron;
no confiemos en vana esperanza;
temamos Aquel que espinas y lanza
azotes y clavos su sangre vertieron.
La su santa faz herida escupieron,
vinagre con hiel fue su potación;
a cada santo lado consintió un ladrón;
nos lleve, le ruego, con los que creyeron. (258)

[Let us forget the vice which caught us thus;
let us not confide in vain hope;
let us fear Him whose blood was spilt
by thorns and lance, scourge and nails.
They spat in His holy wounded face;
vinegar and aloe was his drink,
at each holy side He allowed a thief
we beg Him take us with those who believed Him
(my translation).]

Rojas then transposes a much-revised version of this re-placed stanza to the end of the work as the new closing verses of the *Tragicomedia*. Again the generalized contemplation is made specific and the reader is now exhorted to use the work as a negative example:

Pues aquí vemos cuán mal fenecieron
aquestos amantes, huigamos su danza,
amemos a Aquel que espinas y lanza,
azotes y clavos su sangre vertieron.
Los falsos judíos su haz escupieron,
vinagre con hiel fue su potación;
por que nos lleve con el buen ladrón,
de dos que a sus santos lados pusieron. (st. 1, 236-7)

[Since here we see how badly those
lovers perished, let us flee their dance,
let us love Him whose blood was shed by
thorns and lance, scourge and nails;
the false Jews spat in his face, his
beverage was vinegar and aloe,
may he take us with the good thief of those
two who were placed at his holy sides (my translation).]

Rojas' last stanza before his voice falls silent forever has a distinctly nervous tone:

Y así no me juzgues por eso liviano,
mas antes celoso de limpio vivir;

celoso de amar, temer y servir
al alto Señor y Dios soberano. (st. 3, 237)

[Thus do not judge me loose
on account of this, but rather zealous for
clean living, zealous in loving, fearing
and serving Sovereign God on high (my translation).]

Rojas seems to have altered his purpose in presenting his work; originally the *Comedia* was intended as a type of delicious personal armament against the pains and captivity of love; the *Tragicomedia* he sees more specifically as a didactic and moralistic negative example of the disasters which face those who succumb to lust. This seems strangely contradictory since in the new prologue Rojas tells us that he had expanded the love affair because everyone enjoyed it as fiction and wanted it to last longer: 'miré adonde la mayor parte acostaba, y hallé que querían que se alargase en el proceso de su deleite de estos amantes, sobre lo cual fui muy importunado' (43–4). [I had an eye to mark whither the major part inclined, and found that they were all desirous that I should enlarge myself in the pursuit of the delight of these lovers; whereunto I have been earnestly importuned . . .].

In short, Rojas changed his stated purpose in writing the work from an essentially aesthetic and didactic one in the *Comedia* to an exclusively didactic one in the *Tragicomedia*. In the *Comedia* stanzas the sugared pill will both delight and at the same time cure the love-sick patient:

Como el doliente que píldora amarga
o huye o recela o no puede tragar,
métenla dentro de dulce manjar,
engáñase el gusto, la salud se alarga:
de esta manera mi pluma se embarga,
imponiendo dichos lascivos, rientes,

atrae los oídos de penadas gentes;
de grado escarmientan y arrojan su carga. (st. 5, 38)

[Like the sick man who refuses
a bitter pill or who cannot swallow it:
they put it inside a sweetmeat,
it deceives the taste, and health is regained;
in this way my embarrassed pen,
writing sayings which are lascivious, joking,
attracts the ears of suffering people;
gladly they receive counsel and shed their burdens
      (my translation).]

In the *Tragicomedia* he insists that his didactic purpose is a completely conventional one and he has told this story merely as a negative example of what not to do.

In his new Preface Rojas actually criticizes those who are distracted by the comedy:

otros pican los donaires y refranes comunes, loándolos con toda atención, dejando pasar por alto lo que hace más al caso y utilidad suya. Pero aquellos para cuyo verdadero placer es todo, desechan el cuento de la historia para contar, coligen la suma para su provecho, ríen lo donoso, las sentencias y dichos de filósofos guardan en su memoria para trasponer en lugares convenibles a sus actos y propósitos. (43)

[Others call out the witty conceits and common proverbs, highly commending them, but slighting and neglecting that which makes more to the purpose and their profit. But they for whose true pleasure it is wholly framed reject the story itself . . . and gather out the pith and marrow of the matter for their own good and benefit, and laugh at those things that savour only of wit and pleasant conceit, storing up in their memory the sentences and sayings of philosophers, that they may transpose them into such fit places . . . for their own use and purpose.]

His final verses, 'Concluye el autor' ['the author concludes'], also added to the *Tragicomedia*, repeat this advice to the reader: the work has been flavoured 'con motes y trufas del

tiempo más viejo' [saws and jokes written in olden days].
Rojas' concluding words to the reader are: 'Deja las burlas,
que es paja y granzones, / Sacando muy limpio de entre ellas
el grano' (237) [leave aside the jokes, which are straw and
chaff, /removing the clean grain from within them (my
translation)].

Rojas' intention in this advice to the reader is far from
obvious despite his pervasive repetition. Even the most cur-
sory perusal of *Celestina* discloses that the excellent 'dichos'
which the reader should commit to memory are constantly
used maliciously, satirically and ironically. If we are to
believe any of Rojas' prefatory remarks – and there are those
who would consign the whole lot to the rubbish heap of *topoi*[9]
– then it seems that Rojas may have been explaining his
position to the reader because *Celestina* had been a scandal-
ous success. People either loved it or loathed it because it was
most frequently seen as a funny and bawdy book. As is well
known, a number of the sixteenth-century critics of *Celestina*,
most notably Antonio de Guevara, and Luis Vives in *De
institutione christianae feminae*, I, were scandalized by the work.
Vives, however, modified his opinion somewhat in *De causis
corruptarum artium*, II, and praised the punishment of vice in
the bitter ending of the work. One wonders if, in his
favourable critique in the *Diálogo de la lengua*, Juan de Valdés
could possibly have been referring to the comic beginning
and tragic end when he said: 'me contenta el ingenio del
autor que la començó, y no tanto el del que la acabó' [the
genius of the author who began it pleases me more than that
of the author who finished it].[10] So Rojas' motivation could
have been to defend himself against those readers who
claimed that the book was useless or worse, and to point out
the error of those who enjoyed it for the humour and sex
alone. And he also took the opportunity to correct those
learned readers who wanted to rename the work a tragedy.

Although his pious protestations of didactic orthodoxy may be suspect, his advice to take the book seriously is not. And the conclusion that many contemporary readers did not take the book seriously is inescapable. Perhaps we have gone too far in the opposite direction in this century; in studying the message alone we have overlooked the medium. Tastes in comedy have clearly changed over the past few centuries and what was then considered to be amusing or hilarious may now seem cruel and at times unbearable. Alternatively, we may now need footnotes to explain the jokes to us. There is doubtless a great deal of cruelty in the humour of *Celestina*; the characters poke fun at one another and exploit one another mercilessly. But, oddly enough, we seem to be coming full circle in the twentieth century, in a period when the bulk of humorous fiction falls into the category of black comedy. We may be more sensitive to the blackness than were Rojas' readers, which could well be one reason why he continually warns his reader about the humour in the work, insisting that it is merely a surface coating of sugar. Alonso de Proaza, the book's contemporary editor, may have missed this point himself; his mention in the closing verses of comedy in the work, 'Alonso de Proaza . . . to the reader', simply relates the author to the ancients:

> No dibujó la cómica mano
> De Nevio ni Plauto, varones prudentes,
> Tan bien los engaños de falsos sirvientes
> Y malas mujeres en metro romano. (238)

> [The comic hand of Nevius or Plautus,
> prudent men, did not sketch
> so well the deceits of faithless servants
> and evil women in Roman metre (my translation).]

In fact, he seems to have gone to a rather modern extreme by praising the work principally as a tragedy: 'suplico que llores, discreto lector, / el trágico fin que todos hobieron'

(239). [I beg that you weep, discreet reader, at /the tragic end that they all met (my translation).] As the first critic of *Celestina*, Proaza may well have set the tone for his modern descendants. But we must not forget Rojas' characterization of his own general public; they seem to have read the work as a funny book.

It is hardly surprising, in view of Rojas' change of orientation and the intrusion of his editors' opinions as well, that critics are bitterly divided over the meaning of *Celestina*. The two main schools of thought on the subject may be roughly categorized as the Judeo-pessimistic school and the Christian–didactic school.[11] The Judeo–pessimistic school focuses on Rojas' semitic ancestry and upbringing as a *converso* (descendant from Jewish converts to Christianity), and points out that he must have felt alienated and threatened by his hostile surroundings. They see his outlook as a pessimistic, even nihilistic one, and point out that he turns proverbs and old saws to ironic purpose, criticizing and undercutting the society which is portrayed. Pleberio's lament is often analysed to prove their point.

The Christian–didactic school bases itself on Rojas' claims in the later stanzas, and draws on characterization for support. Calisto is seen as an obvious criticism of the courtly lover (either as a parodic or a tragic figure), and Rojas conveys his moral purpose through a series of familiar medieval *topoi* and conventions.

I should like to propose a return to the text for another consideration of what Rojas tells us about his own work. Essentially, in his prose and verse introduction to the *Comedia* he emphasized two points: first that the story will cure the love-sick, and secondly that it will do this through its beautiful presentation. This sounds like the medieval commonplace about delighting while teaching, and Rojas does in fact refer to the almost-compulsory sugared pill. But it is the delightful quality of the tale which is emphasized: 'aunque dulce cuento, / amantes, que os muestra salir de cativo' (38) [although a sweet story, / lovers, it shows you how to escape from captivity], 'imponiendo dichos lascivos, rientes, / atrae los oídos de penadas gentes; / de grado escarmientan y arrojan su carga' [writing sayings which are lascivious, amusing, / (my pen) attracts the ears of suffering people; gladly they receive counsel and shed their burden (my translation)]. In other words, the story itself will be so delightful and funny to the listeners that they will willingly turn away from the lure of love. In short, Rojas' main emphasis is aesthetic; the sheer delight of listening will cure the listener of his love sickness. Rojas' story in the new verses to the *Tragicomedia* is a very different one. If the listener heeds the dreadful story and the terrible fate of the lovers he will not make the same mistake; no one should accuse Rojas of writing a loose and filthy tale: 'Y así no me juzgues por eso liviano, / mas antes celoso de limpio vivir' (237) [thus do not judge me loose / on account of this, / rather zealous / for clean living . . . (my translation)].

Rojas seems to have taken fright between the first and second editions of his work: 'Unos les roen los huesos que no tienen virtud' (43). [Some gnaw only the bones . . . saying there is no goodness in it.][12] Rojas' social position was certainly not secure enough to withstand accusations that his work was bawdy and less than edifying in tone, and the expanded edition gave him the opportunity to silence these criticisms. This does not stop him, however, from adding a considerable amount of new erotic material to his *Tragicomedia*.

On the basis of the author's own statements, I would therefore like to propose that Rojas' original intentions in completing the *Comedia* were primarily artistic and aesthetic, and that he wished to write a story which would both delight and disenchant suffering lovers. He would accomplish this with two chief artistic weapons, comedy and tragedy. Both the comedy and the tragedy of *Celestina* depend to a large extent on perceptions of contemporary categories of literature. What Rojas and his Salamancan friends found amusing – and occasionally touching – was literary pastiche. *Celestina* is a tapestry of literary allusion and quotation; almost every speech is somehow indebted to a previous literary source, but Rojas dissects these sources, he parodies them, distorts them, satirizes them, and mocks them. His characters are transformations of existing literary clichés, but in their new incarnations they destroy the old conventions and create new ones. A primary target of this process of destruction and recreation is courtly love and the courtly lover. With the figure of Calisto, and to a lesser extent Melibea, Rojas will begin the process of what Bakhtin calls the creation of 'literary' people with their literary way of thinking and their literary way of doing things.

Celestina makes her first visit to Melibea's house; Alisa is called away
unexpectedly to visit a sick relative.

3

Genre and the parody of courtly love

Don Quixote is the first modern novel, according to one of the favourite commonplaces of modern literary criticism. But if one applies to Celestina similar criteria to those that we use for this judgement of Don Quixote, we must accord novelistic priority to the earlier work. Although Bakhtin had worked out some of these criteria when discussing Tirant lo Blanc and Don Quixote in The Dialogic Imagination, he does not seem to have known Celestina. However it fulfils his critera for the 'Second Stylistic Line' novel, which is based on dialogized comic, ironic or parodic discourse, with 'literary' characters who test this discourse by trying to live according to literature.

In Don Quixote Cervantes shows us that it is impossible to live the life of the world of chivalry, that is to say, the world of the medieval romance, in the world of the picaresque. And this is precisely what Fernando de Rojas shows with the figure of Calisto in Celestina one hundred years earlier, since Calisto is a parodic courtly lover, as June Hall Martin has shown.[1] He tries to live the life of a courtly lover of sentimental romance in a dialogic world of prostitutes, servants, pícaros and go-betweens. And, like Quixote, Calisto fails in his attempt and finally dies. Obviously, this is a simplification. There is a great difference between the wise fool Quixote and the erotic egotist Calisto. But their cases are substantially the same, that of the solid citizen whose brains have been scrambled by literary models. Both Rojas and Cervantes destroy the world of the medieval romance by showing that it is impossible to live like an idealized knight-errant or a courtly lover in a picaresque milieu.

What one finds most surprising is the relative absence of anachronism in *Celestina*. While Don Quixote lives the imaginary life of yesteryear, Calisto arrives on the scene only a few years after the success of his model, Leriano of Diego de San Pedro's *Cárcel de Amor*. As E. C. Riley suggested in a recent article on *Don Quixote* and the romance, following Northrop Frye, perhaps the romance did not evolve towards modern fiction; rather there was a deviation of romance towards novel.[2] According to Riley the pure romance may represent the fictional genre in its purest state, while the modern novel could be seen as a realistic corrective. Between 1500 and 1900 fantasy in prose suffers a systematic devaluation at the hands of literary criticism, and the realistic novel dominates in critical opinion, although the romance never disappears. In the twentieth century we are witnessing the resurgence and critical revaluation of the romance.

As Alan Deyermond has suggested,[3] the young Fernando de Rojas discovers an incomplete humanistic comedy with a courtly lover who has comic and parodic potential, and decides to complete this humanistic comedy not as a comedy but as parodic sentimental romance in dialogue, which is at the same time both tragic and comic.

Assuming his ignorance of the existence of the humanistic comedy, the average fifteenth-century reader or listener may have experienced a nervous twinge when Calisto makes his first gushing speech to Melibea in Act I. Was this going to be yet another sentimental romance, set in the slightly unusual form of dialogue? But he did not have long to wait in order to discover that Calisto is a parody of the courtly lover. Even if the reader was unaware of the misuse of Andreas Capellanus in Calisto's approach, Melibea's sarcastic reaction was the clue: 'Pues aun más igual galardón te daré yo, si perseveras' (46). [I shall give thee a reward answerable to thy deserts, if thou persevere and go on in this manner.] Calisto's foolish misunderstanding of her words is soon routed by Melibea's heated clarification of the type of prize that he is to receive if he keeps on pestering her: 'La paga será tan fiera, cual la merece tu loco atrevimiento' (46ff.). [For thy payment shall be as foul as thy presumption was foolish.]

From the first page of *Celestina*, Calisto is the most obvious comic character in the original *Comedia*. The fifteenth-century audience could not possibly have missed this fact after the publishing-business successes of the sentimental romance in the last decade of that century. Yet, astoundingly enough, modern critics overlooked this obvious point until the last few years: Calisto was regarded as a problem hero, unsympathetic and unworthy of Melibea's favour.[4] As recent criticism has pointed out, the primitive author and Rojas both develop and emphasize the parody repeatedly throughout the work. Calisto behaves with characteristic love madness. He is consistently insulted and laughed at by his servants, in asides and to his face. He speaks like a heretic and acts like a madman or a fool.

The primitive author is unrelenting in his presentation of Calisto; his 'hero', a love-besotted nitwit, is an easy mark for dishonest servants and an unworthy lover for a nice girl with a slightly sharp tongue. Rojas will develop Melibea's character in a more sympathetic fashion and will even allow Calisto a more compassionate hearing in the last few acts, perhaps for the sake of credibility. But there is no basic empathy or sympathy in the presentation of the 'hero' to the reader. He is the butt of many jokes in the work, and as such he is unworthy of sympathy or indeed of much character development, beyond his one-dimensional parodic nature. Calisto is a comic character, not a tragic one, although his death does lead to a genuine tragedy in the work, the death of Melibea. When Rojas took over in Act II, it was already too late to redeem Calisto and turn him into a tragic hero. Aristotle's theories of comedy and tragedy are of interest in this analysis:

Aristotle regarded comedy as Tragedy's opposite, a departure from the mean instead of a pursuit of it. He distinguished comedy by ruling that its proper study is men 'worse than the average' – not worse in every way, but worse as regards the Ridiculous (*tò géloion*), which is a subdivision of the Ugly.[5]

Rojas modified the intention of the primitive author, which he contended had been to write a comedy. He could not, however, change Calisto, whose parodic character was too well established to be metamorphosed. This parodic nature was also useful to Rojas, who continued the work under the comic guise. Calisto was too good a joke to be altered or discarded: he provides the comic impetus for Acts VI and XI. If Calisto's character is given a more human dimension after Act XI, this may partially be in an effort to make Melibea's suicide more plausible and more tragic.

My own opinion is that Calisto is a parody, not just of any courtly lover, but of a specific courtly lover, the hero of the Spanish sentimental romance, and most specifically of Leriano, the hero of Diego de San Pedro's *Cárcel de Amor* or *Jail of Love*.[6] Leriano of the *Cárcel* is the archetypal purification of the courtly lover. He is not in fact a typical courtly lover but an extreme case of adherence to the laws of courtly love. This extreme attitude leads to his death at the end of the work. Since he cannot continue the pursuit of his beloved, as that would cause her death and dishonour, he resolves to let himself languish and die of hunger strike or perhaps *anorexia nervosa*. Diego de San Pedro's romance was published in

1492, a scant seven years before our first surviving edition of *Celestina* in the shorter (*Comedia*) version. Rojas possessed a copy of it in his library, according to an inventory made at his death in 1541.[7] There are several verbatim borrowings from the *Cárcel* in the text of *Celestina:* conclusive proof that Rojas knew and had read the *Cárcel*, and probably had it to hand while he was writing *Celestina*.

My theory is that Rojas, who was a student at Salamanca when he wrote *Celestina*, had by then had a surfeit of Lerianos. This would explain various parts of the work which seem incomprehensible if we try to view Calisto as a tragic figure. Calisto is presented as an inept courtly lover from the beginning of the work.

From that very first encounter with Melibea, who rounds on Calisto fiercely, the original author shows us how Sempronio will begin to try to profit from his master's mistakes. The original author's model was not the sentimental romance but the Italian humanistic comedy in Latin, and we have the usual comic plot of the duped master and the canny factotum set in motion. But when Rojas takes over the plotting he sets off in a new direction, that of the tragic sentimental romance. However, his comic Calisto has already been devised, so Rojas makes him a burlesque Leriano. In Act II he is shown alienating his good servant Pármeno by his favouritism towards the bad servant Sempronio. In Act VI he fawns on the bawd and go-between Celestina, and proceeds to exclaim over a *cordón* or girdle which Celestina has obtained from Melibea until even Celestina is disgusted. Throughout Act VI the servants make fun of Calisto's behaviour in sly asides to one another. If Calisto is a tragic hero, as J. M. Aguirre claims, then Act VI is incomprehensible, at least to me. However, after the deaths of both of his servants and the bawd Celestina in Act XII, and after the first night of love in the garden, Calisto does seem to evolve from mere parody to a more interesting and serious figure, one in whom imagination is of paramount importance. In Act XIV he relives his first night of love in his imagination:

Pero tú, dulce imaginación, tú que puedes, me acorre. Trae a mi fantasía la presencia angélica de aquella imagen luciente; vuelve a mis oídos el suave son de sus palabras, aquellos desvíos sin gana, aquel 'Apártate allá, señor, no llegues a mí'; aquel 'No seas descortés' que con sus rubicundos labrios veía sonar; aquel 'No quieras mi perdición' que de rato en rato proponía; aquellos amorosos abrazos entre palabra y palabra, aquel soltarme y prenderme, aquel huir y llegarse, aquellos azucarados besos, aquella final salutación con que se me despidió. (196)

[But thou, my sweet imagination, thou who canst only help me in this case, bring thou unto my fantasy the unparalleled presence of that glorious image. Cause thou to come unto my ears that sweet music of her words, those her unwilling hangings off without profit, that her pretty, 'I prithee leave off; forbear, good sir, if you love me; touch me not; do not deal so discourteously with me?' Out of whose ruddy lips, methinks, I hear these words still sound, 'Do not seek my undoing' which she would evermore be out withal. Besides, those her amorous embracements betwixt every word; that her loosing of herself from me, and clipping me again; that her flying from me and her coming to me; those be sweet sugared kisses, and that her last salutation wherewith she took her leave of me.]

This is from the *Tragicomedia*. Rojas seems to give Calisto a second chance in the additional acts to evolve away from mere parody, although the result is often cowardly and despicable.

I have said that Calisto is specifically a parody of Leriano in the *Cárcel de Amor*. To substantiate this claim with some direct parallels, both Calisto and Leriano use a go-between, both engage in a heated debate over the qualities of women, both die for love. But Leriano uses the discreet Autor of the *Cárcel* for his go-between while Calisto employs the bawd

Celestina. Leriano debates the quality of women gravely with a friend called Tefeo, while Calisto discusses the topic with this faithless servant Sempronio who bests him in the discussion and proceeds to dupe him. And Leriano dies a death of choice and inevitable destiny, while Calisto's death although due to a fatal causality is in its particulars accidental and almost comic – he slips and falls from the wall of Melibea's garden while trying to help his servants, his one act of bravery and one which miscarries. Diego de San Pedro sets out the psychological torment of his hero in the detailed allegory of the *Cárcel* at the beginning of the work; this is paralleled by the portrait which Calisto's servants paint of the sleepless and tormented lover, a portrait which is frankly parodic.

Interestingly enough, Melibea and Pármeno are the two characters who have read the *Cárcel* and know it well enough to quote it verbatim. Melibea answers Celestina's first approach with exactly the same words used by Laureola to reproach the Auctor when he first presses Leriano's suit:

Por cierto, si no mirase a mi honestidad y por no publicar su osadía de ese atrevido, yo te hiciera, malvada, que tu razón y vida acabaran en un tiempo. (95)

[Believe me, were it not that I regarded mine honour, and that I am unwilling to publish to the world his presumptuous audaciousness and boldness, I would so handle thee, thou accursed hag, that thy discourse and thy life should have ended both together.]

Si como eres d'España fueras de Macedonia, tu razonamiento y tu vida acabaran a un tienpo. (*Cárcel*, 96)

[Had you been of Macedonia and not of Spain, your discourse and your life would have ended together.]

The plea of the Cardinal to the cruel king for the life of his unjustly condemned daughter Laureola is the source of two more verbatim quotations. Pármeno pleads for Calisto to listen to his advice about pressing his suit through Celestina, using the Cardinal's words:

más quiero que airado me reprehendas, porque te doy enojo, que arrepentido me condenes, porque no te di consejo. (77)

[I had rather, sir, that you should be angry with me, and reprehend me out of your choler for crossing your opinion, than out of your after-repentance to condemn me for not counselling you to the contrary.]

que más queremos que airado nos reprehendas porque te dimos enojo, que no que arrepentido nos condenes porque no te dimos consejo. (Cárcel, 130)

[We would much rather that you should in your ire reprehend us for angering you more, than that you should when you had repented of your rage, condemn us because we failed to offer you advice.]

Melibea, before her suicide, uses the rationalization of the intemperate king to justify her actions and silence her father:

Porque, cuando el corazón está embargado de pasión, están cerrados los oídos al consejo y en tal tiempo las fructuosas palabras, en lugar de amansar, acrecientan la saña. (229)

[For, when the heart is surcharged with sorrow, the ear is deaf to good counsel; and at such a time good and wholesome words rather incense than allay rage.]

mas bien sabéis cuando el corazón está embargado de pasión que están cerrados los oídos al consejo, y en tal tienpo, las frutuosas palabras en lugar de amansar acrecientan la saña. (Cárcel, 132)

[But you will know that when the heart is possessed by passion, then are the ears stopped against counsel, and at such a time fruitful advice, instead of assuaging, increases rage.]

Like Rojas and unlike Calisto, Melibea and Pármeno are, at the beginning of Celestina, good readers of the Cárcel de Amor who distrust the disastrous effects of courtly passions.

Melibea is also a good critic of a bad courtly lover like Calisto, and Pármeno a good critic of a bad master. But they too are brought to ruin when their passions are allowed to overwhelm their reason, as Melibea recognizes in her closing monologue before her suicide. The primitive author sets up Calisto as the target of his servant's jokes and asides in Act I. Sempronio's reaction to Calisto's music is: 'Destemplado está ese laúd' (48). [This lute . . . is out of tune.] He further comments on Calisto's madness: 'No me engaño yo, que loco está este mi amo' (49) [I was not deceived when I said my master had lost his wits], and on his heresy: 'no basta loco, sino hereje' (ibid.) [madness is not enough; he's a heretic (my translation)]. Celestina takes up the derogatory asides when she first encounters Calisto: 'Sempronio, ¡de aquéllas vivo yo! . . . Dile que cierre la boca y comience [a] abrir la bolsa' (64). [Sempronio, . . . Can I live like this? . . . Bid him shut his mouth and open his purse.] Rojas follows the primitive author's suggestions but manipulates them in a subtler manner. In Act IV, Celestina's descriptions of Calisto to Melibea are both parodic and ironic; we get mock-epic in her description:

en franqueza, Alejandre; en esfuerzo, Héctor; gesto, de un rey . . . De noble sangre, como sabes; gran justador, pues verle armado, un San Jorge. Fuerza y esfuerzo, no tuvo Hércules tanta. (99)

[for bounty, he is an Alexander; for strength an Hector; he has the presence of a prince; . . . nobly descended, as yourself well knows; a great tilter; and to see him in his armour, it becomes him so well, that you would take him to be another Saint George. Hercules had not that force and courage as he hath.]

We proceed from the sublime to the ridiculous in her description of his musical gifts, which, as the audience has already witnessed, are sadly deficient. The fact that Melibea is unaware of the ironies makes these descriptions doubly amusing:

Y el mayor remedio que tiene es tomar una vihuela y tañe tantas canciones y tan lastimeras, que no creo que fueron otras las que compuso aquel emperador y gran músico Adriano, de la partida del ánima, por sufrir sin desmayo la ya vecina muerte. Que aunque yo sé poco de música, parece que hace aquella vihuela hablar. Pues, si acaso canta, de mejor gana se paran las aves a le oír, que no aquel antico, de quien se dice que movía los árboles y piedras con su canto. Siendo éste nacido no alabaran a Orfeo. (99)

[The greatest ease and best remedy he hath, is to take his viol, whereto he sings so many songs, and in such doleful notes, that I verily believe they did far exceed those which that great emperor and musician Hadrian composed concerning the soul's departure from the body, the better to endure without dismayment his approaching death. For though I have but little skill in music, methinks he makes the viol, when he plays thereon, to speak; and when he sings thereunto the birds with a better will listen unto him than to that musician of old, which made the trees and stones to move. Had he been born then, Orpheus had lost his praise.]

Celestina's words to Melibea about Calisto are based on Petrarch's *Epistolae familiares*, 10 and 8:

Quam deditum Musis Adrianum credimus, cujus intentio tan vehemens fuit ut ne vicina morte lentesceret? Prorsus mirum dictu: sub extremum vitae spatium de animae discessu versiculos edidit ... Nec fabulam Orphei vel Amphionis interseram, quorum ille belluas immanes, hic arbores ac saxa cantu permovisse perhibetur.[8]

I suggest that the change of 'Anfion' to 'antico' [ancient] is not merely a misprint as Miguel Marciales has suggested ('antico' for 'Anfieo'),[9] but is intentional on Rojas' part: he suppresses the lesser-known Amphion to emphasize the more familiar Orpheus. This would not have been mere whimsy but is an example of Rojas' turning traditional material to a new purpose. Here, one suspects that he is making a humanistic in-joke for the benefit of his original audience of university friends.

In 1489, several years before Rojas had added his fifteen acts to the original first act of *Celestina*, Marsilio Ficino had published his *De triplice vita* (Florence), the third book of which, *De vita coelitus*, deals with the tempering through music of that influence of Saturn and melancholy which is so common in scholars.[10] To nourish his *spiritus* by absorbing part of the *quinta essentia*, or cosmic spirit, Ficino sang Orphic hymns on his *lyra orphica*. The technique was to imitate musically the character of the god after whom a planet was named, in order to attract jovial, solarian, venerean, or mercurial influences. It is likely that Ficino would have favoured the sun in the tunes played on his *lyra orphica*, probably a *lira de bracchio*, which was adorned with the illustrations of Orpheus charming the animals and rocks. According to D. P. Walker, 'Orpheus was a *priscus theologus* . . . In the series of ancient theologians . . . Orpheus has a conspicuous place, because he is the most ancient of the Greeks, the master of Pythagoras, and through him of Plato. He is also, of course, the symbol of the powerful effect-producing singer, and he was a magician' (23). Walker goes on to suggest that Ficino was the first Renaissance writer to treat the effects of music seriously and practically, although he probably tried to use this Orphic music for magical purposes to invoke some sort of good planetary daemons (48 ff.).

Of course the association of Orpheus and music was an automatic one in the early Renaissance, and there is some evidence that in Spain he was particularly associated with the *vihuela*, a large guitar; an illustration of 1536 in Luis de Milán's *El Maestro*[11] shows Orpheus playing the *vihuela*. But Rojas seems intentionally to have changed Calisto's musical instrument: in Act I he plays the *laúd* or lute, but subsequent references are all to the *vihuela*. Act I also makes explicit reference to the harmony of the spheres and to the fact that Calisto and his lute are out of tune:

¿Cómo templará el destemplado? ¿Cómo sentirá el armonía aquel que consigo está tan discorde, aquel en quien la voluntad a la razón no obedece? (48–9)

[How shall he tune it, who himself is out of tune? Or how canst thou hear harmony from him who is at such discord with himself? Or how can he do anything well, whose will is not obedient to reason?]

However, when Sempronio is asked to sing a sad song, he turns it to a joke about Nero fiddling while Rome burned.

The jokes which Rojas makes at Calisto's expense subsequently are of rather a different sort; I believe that he is combining a sophisticated in-joke about the humanists' Orphic music with the complex ironic contrast of the actual effects of Calisto's music on his soul. Calisto's music, far from transporting his soul to a higher plane or rapture is rather associated with oblivion, sex, and ultimately death and Hell. Yet again Rojas turns a literary topic against itself in order to build a new literary form on the ashes of an old one.

To return to Ficino's theories, Venus is associated with music which is voluptuous, with wantonness and softness; if this sort of music is sung often, the singer's spirit will take on this character.[12] Calisto seems aware that singing love songs will relieve the pain of love; when in the second act Sempronio suggests happy songs (jovial ones?) to divert the mind from thoughts of love, Calisto corrects him: '¿Cómo, simple? ¿No sabes que alivia la pena llorar la causa?' (75). [How like a silly fool thou talkest! Knows't thou not, that it easeth the pain to bewail its cause?]

The subsequent acts in which Calisto is shown singing, VIII and XIII, are heavy with ironies about death and oblivion. In Act VIII, Calisto sings a song attributed to Diego de

Quiñones in the *Cancionero general*: 'En gran peligro me veo; /
En mi muerte no hay tardanza' (139). [In peril great I live,
and straight of force must die.] Sempronio quotes Petrarch,
and Rojas links the obscure Sidonius Antipater with a more
famous poet not mentioned in the Petrarchan text:

El gran Antipater Sidonio, el gran poeta Ovidio, los cuales de
improviso se les venían las razones metrificadas a la boca. ¡Sí, sí, de
ésos es! ¡Trovará el diablo! Está devaneando entre sueños.[13] (139)

[The great Antipater Sidonius or the great poet Ovid, who never
spake but in verse. Ay, it is he; the very same: we shall have the
devil turn poet too shortly: he does but talk idly in his sleep.]

Sempronio's sarcasm here is obvious, since Calisto, far from
composing by improvisation, plagiarizes another's work.
The references to the devil and to oblivion also seem to be
intentional, for after another original and fairly mediocre
stanza, the fact that Calisto cannot tell whether it is day or
night is emphasized:

CALISTO   ¿Es muy noche? ¿Es hora de acostar?
PÁRMENO   ¡Mas ya es, señor, tarde para levantar!
CALISTO   ¿Qué dices, loco? ¿Toda la noche es pasada?
PÁRMENO   Y aun harta parte del día.
CALISTO   Di, Sempronio, ¿miente este desvariado, que me hace
creer que es de día?
SEMPRONIO   Olvida, señor, un poco a Melibea y verás la
claridad. Que con la mucha que en su gesto contemplas, no
puedes ver de encandelado, como perdiz con la calderuela.
(139-40)

[CALISTO   How far night is it? Is it time to go to bed?
PÁRMENO   It is rather, sir, too late to rise.
CALISTO   What sayest thou, fool? Is the night past and gone
then?
PÁRMENO   Ay, sir, and a good part of the day too.
CALISTO   Tell me, Sempronio, does not this idle-headed knave
lie in making me believe it is day?

SEMPRONIO   Put Melibea, sir, a little out of your mind, and you
will then see that it is broad day; for, through that great
brightness and splendour, which you contemplate in her clear
shining eyes, like a partridge dazzled with a buffet, you
cannot see, being blinded with so sudden a flash.]

Calisto is dazzled and blinded, like the partridge who is
hunted by night with lanterns. The partridge, a notoriously
sex-crazed bird[14] according to bestiary lore, would also seem
to be chosen intentionally to symbolize the sex-crazed
Calisto whose music, far from charming wild beasts or lead-
ing his spirit to a higher sphere, seems simply to exacerbate
his own condition of isolation and oblivion.

The connection between this and death is made more
clearly in Act XIII. After his night of love, Calisto's music has
improved markedly. The stanza of *redondillas* (abba) with
quebrados (half-lines) that he sings links strophically and
musically with the end of Melibea's song in Act XIX:

> Duerme y descansa, penado,
> Desde agora,
> Pues te ama tu señora
> De tu grado. (185)

> [Now sleep, and take thy rest,
> Once grieved and pained wight,
> Since she now loves thee best,
> Who is thy heart's delight.]

[But the sleep which he invokes is again a disordered one,
and the oblivion will be brief, since Tristán is about to hear of
the deaths of Sempronio and Pármeno:

TRISTÁN   Señor, no hay ningún mozo en casa.
CALISTO   Pues abre esas ventanas, verás qué hora es.
TRISTÁN   Señor, bien de día.
CALISTO   Pues tórnalas a cerrar y déjame dormir hasta que sea
hora de comer. (185)

[TRISTÁN   There is not so much as a boy in the house.
CALISTO   Open the windows and see whether it be day or no.
TRISTÁN   Sir, it is broad day.
CALISTO   (Close them again); and see you wake me not, till it be almost dinner time.]

In Act XIX the singers seem briefly to achieve that desired effect of Orphic music, but the singers are Lucrecia and Melibea. Calisto receives the benefit of the music, but does not initiate it. Lucrecia and Melibea sing to the stars:

> Estrellas que relumbráis,
> Norte y lucero del día,
> ¿Por qué no le despertáis,
> Si duerme mi alegría? (221)

> [Fair stars whose bright appear
> Doth beautify the sky,
> Why wake ye not my dear,
> If he asleeping lie?]

Calisto seems to be awakened from his slumber at last and his spirit is moved; he exclaims: 'Vencido me tiene el dulzor de tu suave canto; no puedo más sufrir tu penado esperar.' [The sweetness of thy voice hath ravished me; I cannot endure to let thee live any longer in a pained expectation.] When he asks Melibea to go on singing, she answers:

¿Qué quieres que cante, amor mío? ¿Cómo cantaré, que tu deseo era el que regía mi son y hacía sonar mi canto? Pues conseguida tu venida, desaparecióse el deseo, destemplóse el tono de mi voz. (222)

[Why, my love, would you have me sing? Or how can I sing? For my desire of thee was that which ruled my voice and made me to air my notes. But now that thou art come, that desire disappears, it is vanished, and the tone of my voice distempered and out of tune.]

This foreshadows the twentieth act, when the music is replaced by 'este clamor de campanas, este alarido de gentes,

este aullido de canes, este grande estrépito de armas' (229)
[this great noise and ringing of bells, the scriking and cryings
out of all sorts of people, this howling and bark of dogs, this
noise and clattering of armour], which will signal the public
mourning for the death of Calisto.

To return to Rojas' parodic development of Calisto: this
reaches a peak in Act VI when Sempronio, Pármeno,
Celestina, and the audience are alternately bored – or disgusted[15] – by Calisto's excesses over Melibea's girdle, and
amused by the gibes which arise from his behaviour.
Calisto's angry reply to Sempronio's gibe about fondling
Melibea's girdle provokes Sempronio's explanation: 'Que
mucho hablando matas a ti y a los que te oyen. Y así que
perderás la vida o el seso' (115). [Marry, that by talking and
babbling so much as you do, you kill both yourself, and those
which hear you; and so by consequence, overthrow both thy
life and understanding.] This ironic foreshadowing (he has
already lost his wits and will soon lose his life) still does not
silence Calisto, who turns his hyperbolic attentions to
Celestina.

Similar to the parodic portrait of Calisto as courtly lover
are the rôles of both Pármeno and Sempronio in a courtly
double-parody which further devalues Calisto. Sempronio
has Elicia, and Pármeno wins Areúsa, through the cooper-
ation of Celestina in an obvious burlesque parallel to the love
of Calisto and Melibea.

The servants are a grotesque realistic mirror held up to the
love affair of Calisto and Melibea, a love which uses the
highflown rhetoric of the sentimental romance to conceal a
sexuality as realistic as any. The love of Pármeno and Areúsa
is a parody of the love of Calisto and Melibea. Alan
Deyermond points out three occurrences of an *alba* in
Celestina, the first of them parodic, the second and third

serious.[16] In Act VIII, the servant Pármeno and the prostitute Areúsa awaken late in a coarse parody of an *alba*:

PÁRMENO   ¿Amanece o qué es esto, que tanta claridad está en esta cámara?
AREÚSA   ¿Qué amanecer? Duerme señor, que aun agora nos acostamos. No he yo pegado bien los ojos ¿ya había de ser de día? Abre, por Dios, esa ventana de tu cabecera y verlo has. (134)

[PÁRMENO   It is day . . . Whence is it, that it is so light in the chamber?
AREÚSA   What do you talk of day? Sleep, sir, and take your rest; for it is but even now, since we lay down. I have scarce shut mine eyes yet, and would you have it to be day? I pray you open the window by you, the window there by your bed's head, and you shall then see whether it be so or no.]

A serious *alba* is later suggested by the aristocratic lovers, Calisto and Melibea, in Act XIV, after their first night of love:

CALISTO   Ya quiere amanecer. ¿Qué es esto? No me parece que ha una hora que estamos aquí, y da el reloj las tres. (192)

[CALISTO   Is it possible? Look and it be not day already; methinks we have not been here above an hour, and the clock now strikes three.]

This is however a false dawn as Melibea bids him farewell with the words 'y por el presente te ve con Dios, que no serás visto, que hace muy escuro, ni yo en casa sentido, que aun no amanece' (192). [Farewell, my lord: my hope is, that you will not be discovered, for it is very dark; nor I heard in the house, for it is not yet day.]

Deyermond also points out an *alborada* or dawn meeting included in the garden song of Act XIX, the final meeting of the lovers: this is part of the additions to the *Tragicomedia*.

Papagayos, ruiseñores
que cantáis al alborada,

llevad nueva a mis amores,
cómo espero aquí asentada.
La media noche es pasada
y no viene.
Sabedme si hay otra amada
que lo detiene. (221)

[You birds, whose warblings prove
Aurora draweth near,
Go fly, and tell my love
That I expect him here.
The night doth posting move,
Yet comes he not again,
God grant some other love
Do not my love detain.]

Margit Frenk Alatorre has listed these stanzas in her *Lírica
española de tipo popular*, suggesting a popular origin for the
lyric.[17] Even more optimistically, Dionisia Empaytaz has
included two other of the Act XIX songs as possible *alboradas*
in her anthology of Spanish *albas* and *alboradas*:[18]

Estrellas que relumbráis
norte y lucero del día
¿por qué no le despertáis
si duerme mi alegría? (221)

[Fair stars whose bright appears
Doth beautify the sky,
Why wake ye not my dear,
If he asleeping lie?]

This does indeed seem to be the theme of the awakening of
the lover from slumber for a dawn meeting. Empaytaz again
suggests a popular origin for this stanza and for the following
one as well:

¡O quién fuese la hortelana
de aquestas viciosas flores,

por prender cada mañana
al partir a tus amores! (220)

[O that I kept the key,
which opes to these fair flowers,
to pluck them day by day,
When you do leave these bowers!]

The reference to *mañana* [morning] does seem to suggest a dawn love scene again.

The *alborada* is better represented than the *alba* in the Spanish and Galician popular lyric.[19] However, in *Celestina* the meetings of Calisto and Melibea are firmly at night and the intention would seem to be to part well before light in order to avoid scandal. As they leave Melibea's garden after the first night of love, Sosia remarks that they must avoid the very early risers, among them 'Los enamorados como nuestro amo' (192) [love-sick souls, such as our master]. Thus the parodic force of Pármeno and Areúsa's sleep-in until well after dawn. Sosia the stablehand is also scandalized in Act xvii (211–12) by Areúsa's suggestion that Calisto should be preparing for his evening as early as 10 p.m. In Act xiv Calisto prays for long winter nights to set in, then adds:

¿Qué me aprovecha a mí que dé doce horas el reloj de hierro, si no las ha dado el del cielo? Pues, por mucho que madrugue, no amanece más aína. (196)

[What will it benefit me that this clock of iron should strike twelve, if that of heaven do not hammer with it? And therefore though I rise never so soon, it will never the sooner be day].

I would add to this catalogue of night meetings and dawn partings two more significant instances. The first chronologically is in Act xii. There is no hint of an *alba* in the first meeting of Calisto and Melibea in Act xii, which is impeded by the gates of the garden. Calisto does not supply himself with a ladder until Act XIV. However, after the meeting, the two manservants Pármeno and Sempronio go to demand their share of the go-between Celestina's booty, the gold chain which Calisto has given the old hag for her services in procuring Melibea for him. At this stage a savagely ironic *alborada* is suggested:

PÁRMENO   ¿Adónde iremos, Sempronio? ¿A la cama a dormir o a la cocina a almorzar?
SEMPRONIO   Ve tú donde quisieres, que antes que venga el día, quiero yo ir a Celestina a cobrar mi parte de la cadena. (178)

[PÁRMENO   Whither shall we go, Sempronio? To our chamber and to sleep, or to the kitchen and break our fast?
SEMPRONIO   Go thou whither thou wilt; as for me, ere it be day, I will get me to Celestina's house, and see if I can recover my part in the chain.]

When the manservants appear, Celestina comments '¡Oh locos traviesos, entrad, entrad! ¿Cómo venís a tal hora, que ya amanece? ¿Qué habéis hecho?' (179). [O ye mad lads, you wanton wags, enter enter! How chance you come so early? It is but now break of day. What have you done?] When they try to exact their share of the chain, Celestina pretends to have lost it, and enraged, they kill her: following the dawn meeting, we have the most ironic set of dawn partings in the book. As Sosia remarks to Calisto when he tells of the subsequent deaths of Sempronio and Pármeno, who jump from Celestina's window into the arms of the police, 'Pues madrugaron a morir' (187) [But (they) rose too early to their deaths].

The final transformation of the *alba* theme in *Celestina* comes in additional Act XIX, which, as we have already seen, contains possibly three *alborada* references in the lyric poetry sung by Melibea and the servant Lucrecia as they wait for Calisto's appearance in her garden. The dawn imagery is worked into the prose encounter of the lovers. Melibea asks:

¿Dónde estabas, luciente sol? ¿Dónde me tenías tu claridad
escondida? . . . Mira la luna cuán clara se nos muestra, mira las
nubes cómo huyen. (222)

[Where hast thou been, thou bright shining sun? In what place
hast thou hid thy brightness from me? Look on the moon and see
how bright she shines upon us; look on the clouds, and see how
speedily they rack away.]

Calisto brings the scene to a close with the words:

Jamás querría, señora, que amaneciese según la gloria y descanso
que mi sentido recibe de la noble conversación de tus delicados
miembros. (223)

[Oh my dear mistress! I could wish that it never be day that I might
still enjoy that sweet happiness and fullness of content, which my
senses receive in the noble conversing with this thy delicate and
dainty sweet self.]

Calisto replaces the sun, Melibea the moon, and the dawn is
willed away by the lovers. But Calisto will fall to his death
before first light, and Melibea will follow in a suicide just
after dawn, as Rojas tells us in a careful interpolation in
which Pleberio opens a window to let in light so that he can
see the face of his grief-stricken daughter. In my opinion
Rojas not only parodies the *alba* and *alborada* in *Celestina,* but
uses the notion of dawn parting as a cruelly ironic counter-
point to the deaths of the manservants, Celestina, and the
lovers Calisto and Melibea.

Returning to the topic of parody of masters by servants,
Pármeno's reaction to his night of love with Areúsa brings
Sempronio's ironic comment: 'que se eche otra sardina para
el mozo de caballos, pues tú tienes amiga' (136). [I say
nothing but that now you have your wench you will allow
one pilchard more to the poor boy in the stable.] '¿Ya todos
amamos?' (136) [Now I see, we are all in love], he also
remarks dryly in Act VIII. Sempronio himself even manages

to become infatuated with Melibea and himself enters the same game with his enthusiastic questions about Melibea:

Pues dime lo que pasó con aquella gentil doncella. Dime alguna palabra de su boca. Que, por Dios, así peno por sabella, como a mi amo penaría. (105)

[Then tell me what passed concerning that noble lady. Acquaint me but with one word of her mouth; for trust me, I long as much to know her answer as my master doth.]

Celestina's reaction is as violent as it is sarcastic: '¡Calla, loco! Altérasete la complexión. Yo lo veo en ti, que querrías más estar al sabor que al olor de este negocio' (105). [Peace, you fool. What? Does your complexion change? . . . You had rather have the taste than scent of this business.][20] In the banquet scene the comparison of Sempronio with Calisto becomes even more explicit, the alleged cause being Elicia:

aquí está quien me causó algún tiempo andar hecho otro Calisto, perdido el sentido, cansado el cuerpo, la cabeza vana, los días mal durmiendo, las noches todas velando, etc. (147)

[For here is she present who caused me once to become another Calisto, desperate and senseless in my doings; weary in my body, idle in my brain, sleeping ill adays, and watching too well a-nights.]

Elicia berates Sempronio for fancying his master's lady. The two prostitutes then proceed to attack Melibea and they portray her as grotesque and laden with cosmetics, again a parody of the idealized topos of courtly beauty which Calisto has sketched in the first act:[21]

AREÚSA   Pues no la has tú visto como yo, hermana mía. Dios me lo demande, si en ayunas la topases, si aquel día pudieses comer de asco. Todo el año se está encerrada con mudas de mil suciedades. Por una vez que haya de salir donde pueda ser vista, enviste su cara con hiel y miel, con unas tostadas y higos pasados y con otras cosas, que por reverencia de la mesa dejo de decir. Las riquezas las hacen a éstas hermosas y ser alabadas; que no las gracias de su cuerpo. Que así goce de mí, unas tetas tiene, para ser doncella, como si tres veces hobiese parido; no parecen sino dos grandes calabazas. El vientre no se le he visto: pero, juzgando por lo otro, creo que le tiene tan flojo, como vieja de cincuenta años. No sé qué se ha visto Calisto, porque deja de amar otras que más ligeramente podría haber y con quien más él holgase, sino que el gusto dañado muchas veces juzga por dulce lo amargo. (145)

[AREÚSA   O sister! hadst thou seen her as I have seen her (I tell thee no lie), if thou shouldst have met her fasting, thy stomach would have taken such a loathing, that all that day thou wouldst not have been able to have eaten any meat. All year long she is mewed up at home, where she is daubed over with a thousand sluttish slibber-slabbers; all which forsooth she must endure, for once perhaps going abroad in a twelvemonth to be seen: she anoints her face with gall and honey, with parched grapes and figs crushed and pressed together with many other things which, for manners' sake and reverence of the table, I omit to mention. It is their riches, that make such creatures as she to be accounted fair; it is their wealth, that causeth them to be thus commended, and not the graces and goodly features of their bodies: for she has such breasts, being a maid, as if she had been the mother of three children; and are for all the world, like nothing more than two great pompeans or big bottled gourds. Her belly I have not seen, but judging it by the rest, I verily believe it to be so slack and as flaggy as a woman of fifty year old. I know not what Calisto should see in her, that for her sake he should forsake the love of others, whom he may with great ease obtain, and far more pleasure enjoy: unless it be that, like the palate that is distasted, he thinketh sour things the sweetest.]

Of the several third-person portraits of Melibea at least one affords a parodic vision of the courtly 'signs of love'. In Act VI Celestina describes Melibea's reaction to her visit in a grossly exaggerated interpolation:

Y en pos de esto mil amortecimientos y desmayos, mil milagros y espantos, turbado el sentido, bullendo fuertemente los miembros todos a una parte y a otra . . . retorciendo el cuerpo, las manos enclavijadas, como quien se despereza, que parecía que las despedazaba, mirando con los ojos a todas partes, acoceando con los pies el suelo duro. (111)

[And when she had ended . . . she began to fall unto often swoonings and trances . . . full of fear and amazement, all her senses being troubled, (her limbs shaking) one against another . . . writhing and winding her body, her hands and fingers being clenched one within another, like one struggling and striving for life, that you would have thought she would have rent them asunder, hurling and rolling her eyes on every side, striking the hard ground with her tender feet.]

One of the few areas of critical agreement about *Celestina* concerns the author's attacks on love, particularly as articulated by Melibea's father Pleberio at the end of the work in his famous lament. That is to say, almost everyone agrees that Pleberio and by extension Rojas are critical of the misuse of courtly love, although the exact source and focus of Rojas' negative attitude is again an area of disagreement. The Christian–didactic school of *Celestina* studies feels that the criticism is made from a traditional moralistic point of view, whereas the Judeo-pessimistic school sees a much bleaker condemnation of love in Pleberio's words, a pessimistic outlook which holds little hope for human reform or redemption. What is certain is that Pleberio manages to equate love and death in his lament. He exclaims against the God of Love, comparing him with God Almighty, who, he says, only kills what he nurtured while Cupid kills those who follow him:

Dios te llamaron otros, no sé con qué error de su sentido traídos. Cata que Dios mata los que crió; tú matas los que te siguen. Enemigo de toda razón, a los que menos te sirven das mayores dones, hasta tenerlos metidos en tu congojosa danza. (235)

[Some, led with I know not what error, have not sticked to call thee a god; . . . God does but kill those whom he hath created, and thou killest those that do follow thee. O thou, enemy to all reason! To those that serve thee least, thou givest thy greatest rewards until thou hast brought them at last into this thy troublesome dance.] Metaphorical death from love has become real death. The God Love leads the Dance of Death.

Pleberio portrays an inferno of love:

La leña que gasta tu llama, son almas y vidas de humanas criaturas, las cuales son tantas, de quien comenzar pueda, apenas me ocurre. No sólo de cristianos, mas de gentiles y judios, y todo en pago de buenos servicios. (236)

[The sticks which thy flames consume, are the souls and lives of human creatures, which are so infinite and so numberless, that it scarce occurreth unto me, with whom I should first begin; not only of Christians, but of Gentiles and of Jews; and all forsooth in requital of their good services.]

The vocabulary of courtly love, 'servicios' [service] is employed here ironically by the author, in a basic rejection of the effects of the misuse of courtly love. These effects are seen as lethal rather than ennobling. The collision between life and the literary fantasy world of the supposedly courtly lover Calisto and his lady, although initially parodic and comic, leads to the final tragedy of Calisto and Melibea. And although Stephen Gilman has seen the additional *Tragicomedia* night of love as an attempt to salvage something from the human wreckage at the end of *Celestina*, the fleeting compensations of Calisto and Melibea's last tryst make the ending seem all the more tragic.[22] Calisto's ludicrous attempts to ape a courtly lover come to grief in a world of go-betweens, pimps and prostitutes, much as Don Quixote's ersatz knight-errantry will end in a tragic clash of fantasy and reality a century later.

When he discovers the first act of Celestina, an incomplete humanistic comedy, Rojas transforms it into a tragi-comic parody of the sentimental romance, much as Cervantes will write an anti-romance of chivalry a century later. In fact, *Celestina* is a modern novel in dialogue form which damages the antecedent which it parodies. After *Celestina*, the writing of sentimental romances will eventually be abandoned, although they will continue to be read. *Celestina* opens the way for the picaresque genre. As María Rosa Lida de Malkiel has shown in her discarded chapter of *La originalidad artística de 'La Celestina'*,[23] and I have tried to show in my book on memory in *Celestina*, despite its lack of third-person narration, a whole exterior and interior world of realism is revealed in its dialogue form.

4

From parody to satire: clerical and estates satire

Celestina leaves Calisto's house with her bag of gold.

4

From parody to satire: clerical and estates satire

Whether or not there is ecclesiastical satire in *Celestina* has been the subject of some debate in recent criticism.[1] In any event, from the angle of Rojas' contemporary audience various passages seem to fall into this category, whatever the authors' ulterior motives might have been.[2] The primitive author begins this type of satire in a promising vein with Celestina's invention of 'moza' [wench] and 'fraile gordo' [fat friar] to divert Sempronio's suspicions of Elicia's behaviour. Sempronio rises to the bait with his scandal-mongering response:

SEMPRONIO   Por mi vida, madre, ¿qué fraile?
CELESTINA   ¿Porfías? El ministro, el gordo' (57)[3]

[SEMPRONIO   Now, as you love me, good mother, tell me what friar is it?
CELESTINA   Lord, how earnest you be . . . it is that fat friar, (the minister)].

This ecclesiastical satire is amalgamated with estates satire[4] later in Act I on the occasion of Pármeno's multiple description of Celestina:

Asaz era amiga de estudiantes y despenseros y mozos de abades . . .
Subió su hecho a más: que por medio de aquellas comunicaba con las más encerradas, hasta traer a ejecución su propósito, y aquestas en tiempo honesto, como estaciones, procesiones de noche, misas

del gallo, misas del alba y otras secretas devociones. Muchas encubiertas vi entrar en su casa; tras ellas hombres descalzos, contritos y rebozados, desatacados, que entraban allí a llorar sus pecados. (61)

[She was a great friend to your students, noblemen's caterers, and (Abbott's) pages . . . Nay, she proceeded so far, that by cunning means she had access and communication with your very recluses and your votaries and never left them till she had brought her purpose to pass . . . at an honest and holy time, as when they walked their stations, or wend on their night processions, at your midnight masses and your morning matins and such other their secret devotions. Many of them have I seen come into her house disguised and masked because they would not be known. And with them many an holy Friar, bare-footed, breechless, and muffled all over the face, which went thither to bewail their sins.]

The transformation of Celestina's hovel into a convent is ingeniously accomplished.

Rojas enters the arena of ecclesiastical satire modestly, with Elicia's offhand reference to a betrothed girl whose virginity needs restoring when Celestina has been away too late: 'Que has sido hoy buscada del padre de la desposada que llevaste el día de pascua al racionero' (132) [You have been sought after to-day by the father of her that was betrothed, which you brought from the Prebendary upon Easter Day.] This is built up further in Sempronio's description of Celestina to Pármeno at the start of Act IX:

Lo que en sus cuentas reza es los virgos que tiene a cargo y cuántos enamorados hay en la ciudad y cuántas mozas tiene encomendadas y qué despenseros le dan ración y cuál mejor y cómo les llaman por nombre, porque cuando los encontrare no hable como estraña, y qué canónigo es más mozo y franco. (142)

[That which she doth meditate and recite on her beads is how many cracked maidenheads she hath then in cure, how many lovers in this city, how many young wenches are recommended unto her, what stewards afford her provision, which is the more bountiful, and how she may call every man by his name, that when she chanceth to meet them, she may not salute them as strangers, (and which canon is youngest and most generous).]

The climax comes in Celestina's reminiscences about the good old days in the banquet scene. As Américo Castro has pointed out, Celestina's description of her reception at church can be seen, on one level, as a parody of the already parodic 'misa de amor' [love Mass] theme.[5] On another level, it is ecclesiastical satire: . . . 'En entrando por la iglesia, veía derrocar bonetes en mi honor, como si yo fuera una duquesa'. [And when I came to a church, my foot was no sooner in, but I had presently as many bonnets vailed unto me as if I had been a duchess.] She tempers her enthusiastic description of her clerical following somewhat after Sempronio's scandalized reaction, with:

Como la clerecía era grande, había de todos; unos muy castos; otros que tenían cargo de mantener a las de mi oficio. (151)

[As the clergy was great, so I had a great number of them and some of one sort and some of another, some I found very chaste, and some that took the charge upon them to maintain such traders as myself.]

But then she exacerbates the situation again with:

Pues otros curas sin renta, no era ofrecido el bodigo, cuando, en besando el feligrés la estola, era del primero voleo en mi casa. (152)

[Other priests without rents, no sooner was communion offered them, as the parishioners kissed the stole, the bread flew straight into my house (my translation).]

The satirical set-pieces in the work frequently have an identifiable literary source. One of the primary sources is of course the Archpriest of Talavera's *Corbacho*,[6] and one detects an interesting contrast between the primitive author's use of this source and Rojas' own practice. In Act I we find some possible traces of the Archpriest's influence in Sempronio's denunciation of women and in his list of those men who have been made fools by them. There also seems to have been a possible impact on Celestina's imaginative tableau of a love affair which she sketches for Pármeno: 'Esto hice, esto otro me dijo', etc. (71; cf. Castro Guisasola, 172–7). ['this did I do myself; this such a one told me . . .']. Rojas will personalize these anti-feminist satirical pieces from the *Corbacho* and use them for a dual purpose. On the one hand, they are satirical; on the other, they throw new light on the characters speaking them, often an unfavourable light. The set-pieces from the *Corbacho* are concentrated in the banquet scene and in Melibea's reactions to her love for Calisto. Act IX, the banquet scene, is at the same time the most satirical and yet the most pathetic of the acts, as much of the satire rebounds on the speakers. The use of set-pieces from the *Corbacho* would have doubly delighted Rojas' academic audience, but even the general public might have recognized these passages as commonplaces of medieval satire. The verbal attack on Melibea's appearance by Areúsa and Elicia, and Areúsa's denunciation of a servant girl's rôle, fall into categories of well-worn *topoi*: female envy, the attack on cosmetics, and the mistreatment of maids by their mistresses (*Corbacho*, 145–205). Rojas had already prepared the way for the attack on Melibea in Act VI, when Calisto accuses other women of using cosmetics and of being jealous of her:

Pues cuantas hoy son nacidas, que de ella tengan noticia, se maldicen, querellan a Dios, porque no se acordó de ellas cuando a esta mi señora hizo. Consumen sus vidas, comen sus carnes con envidia, danles siempre crudos martirios, pensando con artificio igualar con la perfición que sin trabajo dotó a ella natura. De ellas, pelan sus cejas con tenacicas y pegones y a cordelejos, etc. (117ff.)

[Besides, as many women as are now born, and do know her, curse themselves and complain of God because He did not remember them when He made her, consuming . . . their lives with envy being ready to eat their own flesh for very anger, still augmenting martyrdoms to themselves, thinking to equal that perfection by art, which Nature had bestowed upon her without any labour. They pill and dis-hair their eyebrows with nippers, with plasters of pitch or balm . . .]

When Sempronio echoes this praise of 'aquella graciosa y gentil Melibea' [that fair, lovely, gentle Melibea], Elicia replies in the vein suggested by the Archpriest of Talavera's envious woman, and Areúsa replies by applying the cosmetics topos to Melibea, ending with the *sententia*: 'el gusto dañado muchas veces juzga por dulce lo amargo' (145) [like the palate that is distasted, he thinketh sour things the sweetest]. When Sempronio remarks sarcastically: 'Hermana, paréceme aquí que cada bohonero alaba sus agujas' [Sister, it seemeth here unto me, that every pedlar praiseth his own needles], Areúsa, always with a word of wisdom at hand, replies with Petrarch: 'Ninguna cosa es más lejos de la verdad que la vulgar opinión' (145).[7] [There is nothing farther from truth than the opinion of the vulgar.] Rojas again shows his mastery of the ironic *sententia*, in combination with the satirical portrait.

From the point of view of novelistic discourse, the two prostitutes seem to embody a fairly benign version of the *Corbacho*'s satirical vision of women. That is to say, Rojas pays homage to one of his chief stylistic masters, Alfonso Martínez de Toledo, Archpriest of Talavera, rather than attempting to destroy him. Rojas' use of the *Corbacho*'s acerbic multiple portraits is comparatively kind to the speakers as well: although Elicia at times seems stereotyped in her jealousy and double-dealing, Areúsa receives an altogether more sympathetic portrayal. Her Talaveran diatribe against mistresses and their treatment of maids fits in with her false notion of her own personal freedom, which as we

have seen in Act vii is sharply circumscribed by the occa-
sional presence of her pimp Centurio and the prying eyes of
her neighbours. I quote this important passage at length.

Así goce de mí, que es verdad, que éstas, que sirven a señoras, ni
gozan deleite ni conocen los dulces premios de amor . . . ¡Oh tía, y
qué duro nombre y qué grave y soberbio es 'señora' continuo en la
boca! Por esto me vivo sobre mí, desde que me sé conocer. Que
jamás me precié de llamarme de otrie, sino mía. Mayormente de
estas señoras que agora se usan . . . Y cuando ven cerca el tiempo de
la obligación de casallas, levántanles un caramillo que se echan
con el mozo o con el hijo o pídenles celos del marido o que meten
hombres en casa o que hurtó la taza o perdió el anillo; danles un
ciento de azotes y échanlas la puerta fuera, las haldas en la cabeza,
diciendo: 'Allá irás, ladrona, puta, no destruirás mi casa y honra.'

Así que esperan galardón, sacan baldón; esperan salir casadas,
salen amenguadas; esperan vestidos y joyas de boda, salen
desnudas y denostadas . . . Nunca oyen su nombre propio de la
boca de ellas; sino 'puta' acá, 'puta' acullá. '¿A dó vas, tiñosa?
¿Qué hiciste, bellaca? ¿Por qué comiste eso, golosa? ¿Cómo fregaste
la sartén, puerca? ¿Por qué no limpiaste el manto, sucia? ¿Cómo
dijiste esto, necia? ¿Quién perdió el plato, desaliñada? ¿Cómo faltó
el paño de manos, ladrona? A tu rufián le habrás dado. Ven acá
mala mujer, la gallina habada no parece; pues búscala presto; si
no, en la primera blanca de tu soldada la contaré.' . . . Por esto,
madre, he querido más vivir en mi pequeña casa, exenta y señora,
que no en sus ricos palacios sojuzgada y cativa. (148–50)

[Now I see it is most true, that . . . these forsooth that wait upon
ladies, enjoy not a jot of delight, nor are acquainted with the sweet
rewards of love . . . O aunt! how hard a name it is how troublesome,
and how proud a thing to carry the name of a lady . . . continually
in one's mouth! And this makes me to live of myself ever since I
came to years of understanding and discretion. For I could never
endure to be called by any other name than mine own, especially
by these ladies we have nowadays . . . And when they see the time
draw on, that they be ready . . . for marriage . . . they take occasion
to wrangle . . . with them, and falsely to object unto them, that they

have trod their shoe away . . . either with some one of her ladyship's servants, or with her son, or put jealousies betwixt her and her husband; or that they bring men privily into her house; or that they have stolen such a goblet or lost such a ring: for which . . . bestowing perhaps 100 stripes upon them, and afterwards thrust them out of doors, with their . . . fardles at their backs . . . crying 'Out of my doors, you thief, you whore! . . . Thou shalt not spoil my house, I will not be thus dishonoured by thee.' So that instead of expected recompense they receive nothing but bitter revilements . . . And where they expect to be well married, they are quite marred in their reputation. And where they expect jewels and wedding apparel, there are they sent out naked and disgraced . . . They never hear their own name of their lady's mouth. But . . . 'Come hither, you whore, get you gone, you drab! . . . whither gad you now, you mangy harlotry, you pocky slut? what have you done to-day, you loitering quean? Why did you eat this, you ravening thing? . . . Ah! you filthy sow, how clean this frying pan is kept? . . . why you lazy-bones, did you not make clean my mantle? why said you thus and thus, you sot? . . . Who lost the piece of plate . . . you draggle-tail? What's become of my handkercher, you . . . thief? You have given it to . . . some sweetheart of yours, that must help to make you a whore: come hither, you foul flapse, say, where is my hen, my crammed hen, that I cannot find her? You were best look her me out, and that quickly too, unless you mean I shall make you pay for her, when I come to pay you your wages.' . . . And this, mother, is the reason, why I have rather desired to live free from controlment, and to be mistress in a poor little house of mine own, than to live a slave and at command in the richest palace . . .]

Areúsa's freedom is no greater than that of Lucrecia, who was entering the banquet scene at the time and who may have been meant to overhear Areúsa. Areúsa's 'Que jamás me precié de llamarme de otrie, sino mía' [For I could never endure to be called by any other name than my own . . .] and 'Por esto madre, he querido más vivir en mi pequeña casa, exenta y señora, que no en sus ricos palacios sojuzgada y cativa' [And this, mother, is the reason, why I have rather desired to live free from controlment, and to be mistress in a poor little hovel of mine own, than to live a slave and at command in the richest palace] may have a hollow ring here, but in the 'Tratado de Centurio' Areúsa will in fact declare her independence. Elicia, on the other hand, who has been praised by Celestina for her entrepreneurial spirit and her plethora of admirers, admits in the additional acts that she was always dependent on Celestina's offices, and substitutes Areúsa for Celestina in the 'Tratado de Centurio'.

The Talaveran passages have been analysed by other critics from the angle of each one's rôle in the presentation and development of the characters; what has not been emphasized is their essentially comic nature. It is not too difficult to appreciate a comic diatribe in the mouth of Elicia or Areúsa, but the situation with Melibea is somewhat different. A case in point is Melibea's complaint on the loss of her virginity, which, as Stephen Gilman has pointed out (*Art*, 28–9), is also modelled on a passage in the *Corbacho*. Her lamentations even elicit a sarcastic response from Calisto's servants. Sosia, in an aside, remarks:

¡Ante quisiera yo oírte esos miraglos! Todas sabéis esa oración después que no puede dejar de ser hecho. ¡Y el bobo de Calisto, que se lo escucha! (192)

[You should have sung this song before. Now it comes too late . . . (And that fool Calisto, who listens to it!)]

This brings us to the question, Why is Melibea's loss of virginity funny, particularly at a point when she is being prepared for a tragic end? This is a problem similar to Sosia's remark on Calisto's death, 'tan muerto es como mi abuelo' [He is as dead as . . . my . . . grandfather]: why does Rojas insert comic notes at this point? Is it possible that we, like Calisto, have been looking at Melibea 'with magnifying eyes'? It is a simple enough task for the modern reader to see the tragedy inherent in comedy, but have we lost the capacity to see the comedy inherent in tragedy? This is not to decry Rojas' art but to try to add a dimension that we may have been missing. People may be tragic, but they are also comic; to rob them of half their nature is to impoverish them. Just as we may strive to be noble, virtuous and courageous and are in fact more often lazy, greedy, lustful and cowardly, so we may think that we are tragic when we are in fact comic. Equally, comic elements are an essential part of the chain of causation, both in life and in *Celestina*; tragedy sometimes arises out of comedy. Thus after a comic cowardly interlude Sempronio and Pármeno kill Celestina when she goads them about their cowardice; comedy has become tragedy, but have Sempronio and Pármeno become tragic figures?[28] They definitely have not. It was the tragi-comic nature of man that Rojas must have recognized when he completed and then renamed the *Comedia*; to ignore the ambivalence is to miss the message. As Américo Castro noted, 'Lo nuevo en *La Celestina* . . . es la co-ordinación de su tono gravemente dramático con sus estridencias cómico-grotescas' (110). [What is new in *Celestina* is the balancing of its serious dramatic tone with its comic–grotesque dissonances]. Little did Rojas suspect, when he warned the reader against seeing only the comedy in the work, that one day *Celestina* would face a century of readers who devoured it for its tragic aspects alone. This surely must be the unkindest cut of all, for the redeeming feature of the characters in *Celestina* is their sense of humour. Perhaps it is not always to our taste, perhaps it is cruel and scathing, perhaps the authorial ironies are painful at times. The work's characters may lack omniscience and be unable to laugh at themselves, but they can always see or make a joke at someone else's expense, a virtue or fault they share with their authors. To the modern comic taste this is the one great drawback of humour in the book: the characters act like fools and laugh at one another, but they frequently seem unable to laugh at themselves. But had they always been able to see their own comic faults, we would have been left without a plot. The moments of personal comic insight are rare in *Celestina*. Sempronio makes himself slightly more engaging by telling Calisto to do as he says and not as he does, then he promptly wanders off to be duped by Elicia and Celestina. The latter occasionally lampoons her own *alcahuetería* or rôle as a bawd, even if only as a way of getting at Pármeno: his mother Claudina behaved as badly as she did. But there is great camaraderie in the humour of *Celestina*. The low-life characters defy the upper classes and laugh together at their expense; alternatively, they choose one of their ilk to deceive and dupe. Their obtuseness about their own individual foolishness is part of the work's comedy and tragedy. To ignore this is to ignore one of the most important stylistic and philosophical points of the work. If, as Stephen Gilman suggests, the characters are more like real people than characters, then their comic side is one of the most salient features of their humanity.

5

Verbal humour and the legacy of stagecraft

Pármeno and Sempronio kill Celestina and then throw themselves
from the window as justice approaches; their throats are cut by the
executioner as the alguazil and his men look on.

5

Verbal humour and the legacy of stagecraft

The area of verbal humour in *Celestina* is a complex one, including as it does the use of *sententiae* and old saws, dirty jokes and puns, sarcasm and academic jests, and what has been designated the rise and fall of speech levels, from lofty rhetoric to a more realistic type of speech. Although the latter is not intrinsically comic, it is often used for humorous effect. The ironic use of *sententiae* and proverbs is a field which has been covered by a number of inquiries into *Celestina*.[1] Rojas uses both the aphorisms of the ancients (*sententiae*, *dichos*) and the folk proverbs or old saws (*refranes*) of fifteenth-century Spain ironically, thereby undermining the authority of the speakers who deploy them and the authority of the sayings themselves. As these sayings were the grout which held together the social fabric of medieval Spanish society, the sabotage of this basic material leads to an inversion and collapse of values. Celestina is the chief perpetrator of this attack on received wisdom; she habitually uses aphorisms and old saws to give good advice which will lead to the downfall of her innocent prey Pármeno and Melibea. Rojas exposes the emptiness and treachery of rhetoric and received wisdom in the subversive use of these aphorisms culled from his law books.

Although irony itself is a modern notion, at least in its present definition, the gap between what the characters are saying and what they mean or are trying to perpetrate would have been both obvious and amusing to the fifteenth-century audience. Thus Celestina takes on the cloak of Petrarch and Seneca to win over Melibea and Pármeno. This was no doubt more obvious to Rojas' schoolmates than to the average audience. But they needed no annotated edition to discern the ironies in the use of old saws.

From Act I we notice that the first author is using *sententiae* and old saws with ironic effect. This may include combinations of the two varieties of wisdom. Sempronio welds *sententia* to old saw when he urges that Calisto reward Celestina at once lest she think that he is stalling about payment:

Que no se debe dejar crecer la hierba entre los panes ni la sospecha en los corazones de los amigos, sino limpiarla luego con el escardilla de las buenas obras. (65)

[For it is not good to suffer weeds to grow amongst corn nor suspicion in the hearts of our friends, but to root it out straight with the weed-hook of good works.]

At times this takes the form of an exchange of *sententiae* or old saws, as when Pármeno makes the pseudo-Senecan observation (Castro Guisasola, *Observaciones*, 98) : 'Riqueza deseo; pero quien torpemente sube a lo alto, más aína cae que subió No querría bienes mal ganados.' ['I desire riches, but would not get them wrongfully, for he that rises by unlawful means, falls with greater speed than he got up. I would not for all the world thrive by ill-gotten gain.'] Celestina replies curtly, puncturing Pármeno's self-righteousness:

'Yo sí. A tuerto o a derecho, nuestra casa hasta el techo' (69).

[Marry, sir, but so would I: right or wrong, so as my house may be raised high enough, I care not.]

When Rojas takes up the story, the manipulation of old saws becomes even more skilled. He will split a *refrán* between two speakers for humorous effect, as in Sempronio's question to Celestina about Pármeno's subversion: '¿Cómo has pensado hacerlo, que es un traidor?' [How dost thou think to make him thine? He is a (traitor)]. To which Celestina replies:

'A ese tal dos alevosos' (82)

[For such a crafty knave, we must . . . entertain two traitors for the taking of one].

Rojas also sometimes alters an old saw to allow word-play between two characters, as in Sempronio's remarks to Pármeno about Celestina: Que si anda rodeando su vestido, hace bien, pues tiene de ello necesidad. Que el abad de do canta, de allí viste. [Say she beg her apparel of him . . . she does well in it, having such need thereof as she has. And thou knows't, where the (abbot) sings, there hath he his . . . raiment.] Pármeno replies:

Y aun viste como canta. Y esta puta vieja querría en un día por tres pasos desechar todo el pelo malo, cuanto en cincuenta años no ha podido medrar. (IV, 107)

[(And as he sings, so he dresses) . . . and this old jade would in one day for treading some three steps cast off all her rugged hairs, and get her a new coat; which is more than she could well do these fifty years.]

The original old saw is rhymed: 'El abad de do canta, de allí yanta' [The abbot sings for his supper]. Rojas' ironic use of *sententiae* is marginally more trenchant than that of the original author and is again at times combined with old saws. Pármeno's self-righteousness gets the better of him in Act VII, when he piles up a series of commonplaces for Celestina's benefit:

Verdad es; pero del pecado lo peor es la perseverancia. Que así como el primer movimiento no es en mano del hombre, así el primero yerro; donde dicen que quien yerra y se emienda, etc. (124)

[It is true, but the worser part of wickedness is the perseverance therein, for as the first motion unto sin is not in the power of man to be resisted, so also is it not in the hand of man to avoid once offending. And therefore the proverb tells us, who offends and amends, God will forgive him.]

In this same act, Rojas drags animal imagery into his old saws. The ironic application of the imagery to the animal behaviour of the characters is particularly noticeable when Pármeno and Celestina go to Areúsa's house. Thus Celestina deletes the *asno* [ass] from the old saw when she says to Areúsa: 'Otro es el que ha de llorar las necesidades, que no tú. Hierba pace quien lo cumple' (126) [let others bewail their wants, not thou. Herbs feed them that gather them], for 'asno pace' [an ass grazes]. She continues in this same vein with:

No atesores tu gentileza, pues es de su natura tan comunicable como el dinero. No seas el perro del hortelano. (127)

[Do not, like a miser, hoard up your beauty . . .; silence in its own nature is as communicable . . . as money . . . Be not her mastiff in the garden, nor the dog in the manger.]

Animals and the devil get mixed up in one of her remarks to Pármeno:

Llegáte acá, asno. ¿Adónde te vas allá asentar al rincón? No seas empachado, que al hombre vergonzoso el diablo le trajo a palacio. (130)

[Come hither, you ass, whither go you now, to sit moping down in a corner? Come, come, be not so shamefast, for it was the bashful man whom the devil brought to court . . .]

The devil here would seem to be Celestina herself. Celestina's dialogic persona and her terrifying deployment of *sententiae* and old saws to pervert and corrupt strike me as being a parody of a bad legal practice. Her powers to disrupt through rhetoric have been convincingly demonstrated by

George Shipley, Malcolm Read and Leslie Turano.[2] Nothing seems to be sacred to Rojas, not even his own profession, which is here categorized as a division of rhetoric, or literature as we now call it. Celestina's behaviour is a powerful condemnation of the ability of language, literature and received wisdom to be used as a tool to corrupt and debase. The comic picture of the old bawd who convinces through sophistry and amuses with her distorted use of received wisdom is easily transformed into a sinister vision of an evil creature who uses her linguistic powers to corrupt and eventually destroy. The fact that she falls prey to her own evil powers – hurling abusive aphorisms at Sempronio and Pármeno long after she should have thought to shut her mouth – shows the self-destructive nature of Celestina's gifts.

Rojas uses the same technique of the ironic use of *sententiae* in the additional acts. When Areúsa compliments the dupe Sosia by saying: 'quien bien quiere a Beltrán a todas sus cosas ama' in Act XVII (211) [he that loves Beltran loves anything that is his], she is implying that Sosia is comparable to a dog; the full reading of the refrán is: 'Quien quiere a Beltrán, quiere a su can' [who loves Beltran loves his dog]. The culmination of this ironic use of old saws is in the tragic dénouement, and the use of risible commonplaces in the face of disaster. Thus Sosia reacts to his master's death with two old saws: '¡A esotra puerta! ¡Tan muerto es como mi abuelo!' (224) [Let us call a little at this other door. He is as dead as . . . my . . . grandfather]. And even Pleberio, the most serious figure in the work, cannot initially rise above the trivial 'Nuestro gozo en el pozo' (XXI, 232) [Our solace is in the suds] after witnessing his daughter's death.

In the area of verbal obscenities, we might note that there are surprisingly few of these in *Celestina*, particularly considering the fact that the 'obras de burlas' [humorous poems] in the *cancioneros* or songbooks were replete with filthy language. The dirty jokes in *Celestina* are of a subtler nature, although overtly sexual. The primitive author seems to have had more bawdy tastes than Rojas. Aside from Sempronio's reference to the famous case of Calisto's granny and the monkey,[3] we find the exchange between Celestina and Sempronio: 'Pocas mataduras has tú visto en la barriga'; 'Mataduras no; mas petreras sí' (57) [You have seen few saddlesores on the stomach! You don't mean saddlesores, but breastplate sores! (my translation)] and Celestina's joke about Pármeno's 'cola de alacrán' [tail of a scorpion]: 'Y aún peor: que la otra muerde sin hinchar y la tuya hincha por nueve meses' (66), [for that other stings without swelling, and thine swells for nine months together] which raises a 'Hi, hi, hi' from Pármeno. The primitive author's altogether more jolly outlook on life is confirmed by the exchange between Sempronio and Calisto about the latter's lust being worse than that of the people of Sodom, 'Porque aquéllos procuraron abominable uso con los ángeles no conocidos y tú con el que confiesas ser dios'. [For they did but go about to procure abominable use with angels whom they knew not, and thou with her whom thou confessest to be a god]. Calisto laughs against his will: '¡Maldito seas! Que hecho me has reír, lo que no pensé ogaño' (51) [A pox on thee for a fool, thou makest me laugh, which I thought not to do today].

Rojas seems to have less taste for bawdy remarks, but more taste for comic erotic scenes, such as Act VII, Celestina's attempt to arouse both the inexperienced Pármeno and the supposedly reluctant Areúsa to sexual frenzy with her erotic comment on Areúsa's appearance.[4] In fact, his attempt to work some obscene humour into this act fails rather dismally, and he repeats his only rude joke in an interpolation. Celestina remarks to Areúsa: 'No espero mas aquí yo, fiadora que tú amanezcas sin dolor y él sin color' (131) [I will stay no longer with you, and I will warrant you . . . that you shall rise tomorrow without pain and he pale . . . without colour], and a variant of this is interpolated in an earlier remark to Areúsa: 'Y si no crees en dolor, cree en color' (128) [and if you don't believe in pain believe in colour (my translation)]. Hence our surprise at Calisto's apparent lapse of good taste in Act XIX when he suddenly blurts out: 'Señora, el que quiere comer el ave, quita primero las plumas' (223). [Madame, he that will eat the bird must first pluck the feathers.] But more of these comic incongruities later.

Puns occur but occasionally in *Celestina* and rather nervously at that. There is an ingenious one in Act III when Sempronio transforms the old saw: 'Ir por lana y volver trasquilado' [go for wool and return shorn] into 'no vayas por lana y vengas sin pluma' [Go not to fetch wool . . . And come back yourself without your plumes]. '¿Sin pluma, hijo?' [Without my plumes, my son?], asks Celestina. 'O emplumada, madre, que es peor' [Or rather implumed mother, which is worse], replies Sempronio (84). This does not make Celestina laugh, or even groan; she becomes angry.

The rise and fall of speech levels has been studied by Carmelo Samonà and Stephen Gilman,[5] but one might point out a few instances in which this produces a primarily comic effect. The puncturing of Calisto's inflated speeches was begun by the primitive author with Melibea's sarcastic reaction to the protagonist's first speech. Calisto's encomium of Celestina when she first appears draws a cynical and violent aside from Celestina: 'Sempronio ¡de aquéllas vivo yo!' (64). [Sempronio, can fair words make me the fatter? Can I live by this?].

Rojas develops this line of humour when both Calisto and Melibea (160ff.) adopt an inappropriate reverential tone towards Celestina. For example, Calisto's high praise in the sixth act is punctured first by Celestina: 'Señor, no atajes mis razones; déjame decir, que se va haciendo noche' [Sir, do not stop me in the course of my speech. Give me leave to go on, for night draws on], and then by Pármeno's sarcastic aside at her request to be accompanied home: '¡Sí, sí, porque no fuercen a la niña!' (112). [O yes, in any case! Because she is young . . . and may chance to be ravished by the way]. Celestina picks up this joke at her expense later in Act VII: 'que yo vieja soy; no he temor que me fuercen en la calle' (132) [for I am old, and therefore fear not to be forced in the streets], then overworks it in Act IX when she calls to the girls and pretends that Sempronio and Pármeno are about to attack her: 'que están aquí dos hombres que me quieren forzar' (143) [for there are a couple of young gallants that would ravish me]. The ironic foreshadowing of her death is fairly obvious.

Calisto's own rise and fall in tone, highly inappropriate in an alleged courtly lover, has been pointed out by June Hall Martin (*Love's Fools*, 100ff.). Thus, in the first act he berates Sempronio for idling on the job directly after returning from his encounter with Melibea (47); later Pármeno receives the same rough treatment. Celestina is far more clever in her use of rhetoric, and the tone usually drops before she reaches the end of a long speech. Thus, in Act VII she rambles on to Pármeno about the wisdom of age and the virtues of friendship until she hits on his weakness:

Oh ¡cuán dichosa me hallaría en que tú y Sempronio estuviésedes muy conformes, muy amigos, hermanos en todo, viéndoos venir a mi pobre casa a holgar, a verme y aun a desenojaros con sendas mochachas! (121)

[Oh! how happy should I be, might I but see thee and Sempronio agree, see you two friends and sworn brothers in everything, that ye may come to my poor house to be merry, and to see me now and then, and to take your pleasure with (both your wenches).]

To Pármeno's '¡Mochachas, madre mía?' [Wench(es), mother?] she replies: '¡Alahé! Mochachas, digo; que viejas,

harto me soy yo' (121). [Ay wench(es), and young one(s) too
– as for old flesh, – myself am old enough.] In Act v, after
having wheedled the girdle from Melibea, she replies to
Sempronio's advice about not telling Calisto the good news
too soon with a long philosophical piece that ends: 'Calla,
bobo, deja hacer a tu vieja' (105). [Peace, you fool, let . . .
your old woman . . . handle him.] At times Celestina even
parodies her own high style, as when she refuses to tell
Sempronio about her success with Melibea: 'Que será
desflorar mi embajada comunicándola con muchos' (103).
[For by communicating myself to many, I should as it were
deflower my embassage.]

One final area of verbal humour in *Celestina* might be
designated somewhat anachronistically 'college humour'.
These are jokes for Rojas' academic audience, and they fall
into several categories. For example, there is parody of
Biblical style, as when Pármeno murmurs in an aside: 'Paz
con Sempronio. La paz no se debe negar; que bienaventurados son los pacíficos, que hijos de Dios serán llamados' (72).
[To be at peace with Sempronio; and to peace no man ought
to be opposite, for blessed are the peaceful for they shall be
called the children of God.] This one would have been
obvious to the general audience as well. One also suspects a
lampoon of the church in Celestina's description of
Melibea's girdle: 'que es fama que ha tocado todas las
reliquias que hay en Roma y Jerusalén' (97). [For the report
goes it hath touched all the relics that are in Rome and
Jerusalem.] Scholastic jokes are somewhat less obvious
although parody is frequent, as when the love-maddened
Calisto asks Pármeno the Petrarchan question: '¿No sabes
que el primer escalón de locura es creerse ser sciente?' (77).[6]
[consider with thyself that the first round in folly's ladder is
for a man to think himself wise.] School slang seems to be
carefully explained in an interpolation, when Celestina re-

fers to Sempronio: 'tirando a pájaros y aojando pájaras a las ventanas. Mochachas digo, bobo, de las que no saben volar, que bien me entiendes' (104) [shooting at birds, aiming at other birds with your eye, that take their standing in windows. I mean pretty wenches, you fool, such birds . . . as have no wings to fly from you: you know my meaning, sir]. This one has come full circle, and we no longer need an explanation to understand it, at least not in English. Finally there is Rojas' academic joke about scribal errors, also interpolated in the original text. Pármeno remarks: 'Madre, pues tres veces dicen que es bueno y honesto todos los que escribieron' [thrice . . . is good . . . and all that do write thereof, do allow you no more], and Celestina answers: 'Hijos, estará corrupta la letra: por trece, tres' (144).[7] [Son, the phrase is corrupted; they have put three times instead of thirteen.]

Pármeno and Sempronio often play the rôle of parodic students in the work. Pármeno excells in garbled Aristotle: 'No curo de lo que dices, porque en los bienes mejor es el acto que la potencia y en los males mejor la potencia que el acto' (66) [I regard not what thou sayest. For in good things, better is the act than the power; and in bad things, better the power than the act], and Sempronio in garbled authorities and mythology ('¿No has leído de Pasife con el toro, de Minerva con el can?') (51). [Have you not heard of Pasiphae, who played the wanton with a bull? and of Minerva, how she dallied with a dog?][8] With their parodic discourse they unconsciously satirize their master in both his courtly and student rôles, although at times they will mock him consciously as well.

Verbal humour, although of necessity an artificial and wide-ranging category, includes some of the most important facets of humour in *Celestina*. The ironic use of old saws and *sententiae* to devalue the received wisdom of the ages has been noted by previous critics. Perhaps more disturbing are the incongruities in the use of old saws and jokes in the work: trivial, silly, even risible lines appear at tragic moments. Rojas might be accused of trivializing his subject matter, but the underlying reason for this technique seems rather to be related to his basic view of mankind.

The legacy of stagecraft

The Salamanca audience was obviously well versed in the traditions of Roman and humanistic comedy, although the general public probably knew little about these traditions. However, the primitive author made certain that the public were well aware of the humorous stage devices borrowed from Latin antecedents and he never used an aside without forcing the issue: X was mumbling to himself, Y queried it, and X made up some similar-sounding nonsense to appease Y. In case they still managed to miss the point, Proaza gave reading directions in his closing stanzas: 'Si amas y quieres a mucha atención / Leyendo a Calisto mover los oyentes, / Cumple que sepas hablar entre dientes' (238). [If you love and wish to move the listeners to great attentiveness while reading Calisto, it is necessary to know how to speak in asides ... (my translation).] This passage also underscores the fact that *Celestina* is a piece designed not for theatrical production, but to be read aloud to an audience. In the first act the aside is introduced immediately with Sempronio's irreverent descant on his master's raptures over Melibea. At the opposite end of the spectrum in Act I we find Celestina speaking loudly so as to be intentionally overheard when she turns up on Calisto's doorstep. She previously had warned Elicia of Sempronio's arrival with the same device in the Crito scene.

When Rojas takes up the aside, the humour will be even subtler. Pármeno's asides in Act II are not only amusing but also ominous, since they foreshadow the course of the action:

'dime si lo hecho apruebas' [tell me whether thou approvest of what I have done or no] brings the aside: '¡Apruébelo el diablo!' (76) [the devil approve it].

Celestina herself will indulge in asides to the devil in Act IV (90, 95), and Lucrecia's own perception of diabolism in the old hag will cut across Celestina's asides: '¡Hi, hi, hi! ¡Mudada está el diablo! ¡Hermosa era con aquel su Dios os salve que traviesa la media cara!' (92). [She changed? Hi, hi, hi! the devil she is: she was fair when she met with him that scotched (scarred) her over the nose.] Celestina's diabolism is the excuse for a humorous or bitter aside on various occasions, as in Areúsa's: '¡Válala el diablo a esta vieja, con qué viene como huestantigua a tal hora!' (126). [Now the devil take this old trot! What news with you, that you come thus stealing like a ghost, and at so late an hour?]

Rojas often uses interchanges between servants to punctuate and puncture more serious scenes, as in Pármeno and Sempronio's running commentary on Calisto and Celestina's interview in Act VI. Their cowardly and burlesque dialogue also punctuates the first interview between the lovers in Act XII.

There is heavy sarcasm in most of Rojas' asides; Celestina's remarks against Melibea in Act X are especially brutal: 'Tú me pagarás, doña loca, la sobra de tu ira' (154) [I will be even with you, you fool, for your yesterday's anger]. She counters Lucrecia's accusations of diabolism with her own: 'Nunca me ha de faltar un diablo acá y acullá: escapóme Dios de Pármeno, topóme con Lucrecia' (157). [One devil or other is still haunting me, one while here, another while there. I have escaped Pármeno, and have fallen upon Lucrecia.] But Lucrecia has the final word and the final aside in this scene when she remarks dryly of Alisa's forgetfulness: 'Tarde acuerda nuestra ama' (162). [My old lady's counsel comes too late.]

Asides are sometimes combined with other elements of stagecraft for additional effect. For example, in Act VI we get the bonus of visual humour. Pármeno and Sempronio are bored by Calisto's effusions to Celestina and start gesticulating to Celestina to end the interview; while Calisto rants on, Celestina manages to whisper to them without being overheard: 'Bien te entiendo, Sempronio. Déjale, que él caerá de su asno y acabará' (118). [Sempronio, I understand your meaning; but give him leave to run on; for he will fall anon from his ass, and then his journey will be at an end.] Asides alternate with rapid dialogue on other occasions; thus in Act VIII, when Sempronio and Pármeno plan to steal food for their banquet:

CALISTO ¿Quó dices, Sempronio?
SEMPRONIO Dije, señor, a Pármeno que fuese por una tajada de
    diacitrón.
PÁRMENO Hela aquí señor.
CALISTO Dacá.
SEMPRONIO (Verás qué engullir hace el diablo. Entero lo quiere
    tragar por más apriesa hacer). (141)

[CALISTO What sayest thou, Sempronio?
SEMPRONIO I speak, sir to Parmeno, that he should run and
    fetch you a slice of conserves of citron.
PÁRMENO Lo, sir, here it is.
CALISTO Give me it hither.
SEMPRONIO See, how fast it goes down! I think the devil makes
    him make such quick work. Look, if he does not swallow it
    whole, that he may the sooner have done!]

One final and sophisticated use of the aside is in Act XVI, when Melibea and Lucrecia conduct a secret conversation while her parents are discussing Melibea's future. Here Melibea intentionally satirizes her parents' remarks on her supposed virginity.

Rojas also exploits the comic potential of scenes in which

the characters observe one another. Celestina is the favourite object of everyone's observation, and the commentary involves a sharp contrast to the form of address the characters usually adopt towards 'madre Celestina'. Sempronio exclaims: '¡Qué espacio lleva la barbuda; menos sosiego traían sus pies a la venida!' (III, 79). [Look what leisure the old bearded bawd takes! How softly she goes!] In the realm of visual humour, the superstitions of the characters are also risible. Lucrecia's blushing reluctance to name the witch Celestina is laughed at by Alisa, although the joke will finally be on Alisa herself (89). Pármeno also shows superstitious fear of Celestina when he crosses himself in her presence (109). Even Melibea's dead faint at the sound of Calisto's name has a comic side when the frantic Celestina tries to revive her (159).

In the area of characterization, much has already been written on the subject of the characters' relation to the Roman stage and the humanistic comedy. The general public would not have been as familiar with *Celestina*'s cast of characters as the educated readers; the lover, the beloved, the go-between, the servants, the *lena*, were all well-established theatrical figures. And when the *miles gloriosus* showed up in the additional acts in the uncharacteristic guise of a pimp, the hilarity must have been considerable. Significantly, Centurio is largely a stereotype, unlike the rest of the characters. He therefore fails to fit into the pattern of novelistic dialogic discourse in the work. His incongruity has been felt but never before expressed in this manner; perhaps the fact that he seems not to belong to the work has contributed to current theories that the 'Tratado de Centurio' is by another hand.[9] More interesting than this borrowing of stereotypes is the use of traditional comic characterization by both authors. The duping of Sempronio by Elicia in Act I and of Sosia by Areúsa in the additional acts are both cases in point; significantly, the latter duping is less pleasant and more vindictive than the former.

Curiously, the influence of comic stagecraft on *Celestina* seems to be slight; or perhaps this is to be expected in a work that was never destined for the stage. In Act I the only sequence which depends heavily on action for humour is the third scene, when Sempronio arrives unexpectedly at Celestina's house and Elicia must be warned in time to get rid of Crito. Another comic-action scene takes place in Act XII when Pármeno and Sempronio flee their imagined enemies and then return shamefaced to their job of guarding the lovers. Verbal set-up jokes are even rarer. Elicia plays Centurio's straight-man in an etymological joke in Act XVIII when she asks him how his grandfather earned his name by his sword: 'Dime, ¿por ventura fue por ella capitán de cient hombres? *Centurio* No, pero fue rufián de cient mujeres' (216). [Was he by it made captain of a hundred men? *Centurio* No, he was made it by (procuring) to an hundred women.] This lack of actable scenes, along with the average length of many speeches, provides more textual evidence that even as a comic work *Celestina* was meant to be read rather than acted. There are, on the other hand, a number of scenes of lively dialogue which Castro Guisasola (*Observaciones*, 80–94) listed as possible borrowings from Terence, or as showing his influence. Besides the Crito scene, some of this rapid dialogue serves an excellent comic purpose, e.g., in the case of the exchange between Celestina and Pármeno about Areúsa, where repetition is used to humorous effect:

PÁRMENO   ¿De Areúsa?
CELESTINA   De Areúsa.
PÁRMENO   ¿De Areúsa, hija de Eliso?
CELESTINA   De Areúsa, hija de Eliso.
PÁRMENO   ¿Cierto?
CELESTINA   Cierto.

PÁRMENO   Maravillosa cosa es.
CELESTINA   Pero ¿bien te parece?
PÁRMENO   No cosa mejor. (70)

[PÁRMENO   To Areusa?
CELESTINA   Ay, to Areusa.
PÁRMENO   To Areusa, the daughter of Eliso?
CELESTINA   To Areusa, the daughter of Eliso.
PÁRMENO   Is this certain?
CELESTINA   Most certain.
PÁRMENO   It is marvellous strange.
CELESTINA   Dost thou like (it)?
PÁRMENO   Nothing in the world more.]

Another area of facetious characterization suggested by the primitive author and exploited by Rojas is that of comic cowardice. Sempronio's cowardice is suggested in Act I when he at first expresses dismay and fear at his master's infatuation and then determines to exploit it:

¿Dejarle he solo o entraré allá? Si le dejo, matarse ha; si entro allá, matarme ha. Quédese; no me curo; más vale que muera aquél, a quien es enojosa la vida, que no yo, que huelgo con ella. (48)

[Shall I leave him all alone, or shall I go in to him? If I leave him alone, he will kill himself. If I go in, he will kill me. Let him bide alone and bite upon the bit, come what come, I care not. Better it is that he die whose life is hateful unto him, than that I die, when life is pleasing unto me.]

In Act XII Rojas will explore the humorous possibilities of Sempronio and Pármeno's cowardice to the fullest extent in the garden scene. First they voice their fears, then they run away gratuitously; next they try to impress one another with their past feats of courage; finally they try to impress Calisto with their bravery.

SEMPRONIO   ¿Dormir, señor? ¡Dormilones son los mozos! Nunca me asenté ni aun junté por Dios los pies, mirando a todas

partes para, en sintiendo, poder saltar presto y hacer todo lo
que mis fuerzas me ayudaran. (178)

[SEMPRONIO Sleep, sir? It is for boys . . . to sleep; I did not so
much as once sit down, nor put one leg over another, watching still as diligently . . . that if I had heard but the least noise . . .
I might presently have leapt forth and have done as much as
my strength should have been able to perform.]

This comic crescendo suddenly turns to tragedy when they
attempt to bluff Celestina as well; she confronts them with
their cowardice and they kill her. '¿Con una oveja mansa
tenéis vosotros manos y braveza? ¿Con una gallina atada? . . .
Señal es de gran cobardía acometer a los menores y a los que
poco pueden' (183). [Shall your valour and your bravings be
exercised on a poor silly innocent sheep? On a hen that is tied
by the leg . . .? . . . It is an infallible note of cowardice, to assail
the weak and such as have . . . little power to resist.] A
parallel case, although not such a comic one, is Calisto's
poltroonery after the death of his servants, which contrasts
with the bravery that leads to his own death:

Oh triste yo; ¿cuándo se restaurará tan grande pérdida? ¿Qué
haré? ¿Qué consejo tomaré? ¿A quién descubriré mi mengua? ¿Por
qué lo celo a otros mis servidores y parientes? Tresquílanme en el
concejo y no lo saben en mi casa. Salir quiero; pero, si salgo para
decir que he estado presente, es tarde; si ausente, es temprano.
(194)

[O miserable that I am, when shall I recover so great a loss? What
shall I do? What counsel shall I take? To whom shall I discover my
disgrace? Why do I conceal it from the rest of my servants and
kinsfolk? They clip and note my good name in their council-house .
. . and they of mine own house and kindred must not know of it. I
will out amongst them: but if I go out and tell them that I was
present, it is too late; if absent, it is too soon.]

Señora, lo que no hace espada y capa y corazón, no lo hacen
corazas y capacete y cobardía. (224)

[That, mistress which a sword, a cloak, and a good heart cannot do, can never be effected by cuirass, casque, or cowardice.]

Again we find incongruous blends of comedy and tragedy, which cannot be ignored. These combinations are inseparable: Celestina's death, stabbed by her accomplices, is mock-heroic (reminiscent of the death of Julius Caesar). Alonso López Pinciano in fact claims that the death of an *alcahueta* is essentially comic:

& ansí las muertes trágicas son lastimosas, mas las de la comedia, si alguna ay, son de gusto y passatiempo, porque en ellas mueren personas que sobran en el mundo, como es una vieja zigañadora, un rufián o una alcahueta[10]

[thus tragic deaths are pitiful, but those in comedy, if they occur, are pleasant and amusing, because unnecessary people die, such as an old gossip, a procurer, or a go-between.]

Calisto's death by falling from a ladder, though not, strictly speaking, comic, is a base and trivial one. And the comic cowardice conducive to Celestina's death and ultimately to the death of the lovers demonstrates how inseparable are comedy and tragedy. This interlacing of comic and tragic elements is far more skilful in *Celestina* than in its continuations: Pierre Heugas gives some idea of their shortcomings in comedy.[11] This brings us to our final topic: the rhetorical shift from comedy to tragedy and its relation to novelistic discourse.

6

The rhetorical shift from comedy to tragedy: ironic foreshadowing and premonitions of death

---

Calisto sleeps while Sosia tells Tristán the news of the deaths of
Pármeno, Sempronio and Celestina.

6

The rhetorical shift from comedy to tragedy: ironic foreshadowing and premonitions of death

According to a commonplace of *Celestina* criticism, the characters all have premonitions of their impending deaths and of the disasters which occur at the end of the work.[1] The technique of foreshadowing in the *Comedia* can be divided into three categories: (a) general theories of death, (b) premonitions of their own deaths and predictions of the deaths of others, and finally (c) imprecations containing prophecies of death and ironies unknown to the speaker.

Erna Ruth Berndt, in her book *Amor, muerte y fortuna en 'La Celestina'*,[2] considered Celestina to be the mouthpiece of a generalized philosophy of death, citing in particular her famous exclamation against death: '¡Oh muerte, muerte! A cuántos privas de agradable compañía . . . Por uno que comes con tiempo, cortas mil en agraz' (III, 81). [O death, death, how many dost thou deprive of their sweet and pleasing society! . . . For one that thou eatest being ripe, thou croppest a thousand that are green.] Celestina points out the unexpected nature of death with the aphorism: 'Ninguno es tan viejo, que no pueda vivir un año, ni tan mozo, que hoy no pudiese morir' (IV, 92). [There is no man so old but he may live one year more, nor no man so young but he may die today.] Elicia also contemplates death philosophically and uses the well-known topic of death the leveller as the justification for her Epicurean philosophy:

83

También se muere el que mucho allega como el que pobremente
vive, y el doctor como el pastor, y el papa como el sacristán ... No
habemos de vivir para siempre. Gocemos y holguemos, que la vejez
pocos la ven y de los que la ven ninguno murió de hambre. (VII,
133).

[As well dies he that gathers much as he lives but poorly, the doctor
as the curate, the poor as the sexton, we are not to live for ever for
few are they that come to see old age; and they who do see it, seldom
die of hunger.]

As usual, Pármeno is the character who has the clearest
vision of the transitory quality of life and the inadequacy of
living for today; instinctively he seems to foresee the tragic
outcome of the amorous comedy that they all act:

A los alegres, serenos y claros soles, nublados escuros y lluvias
vemos suceder; a los solaces y placeres, dolores y muertes los
ocupan; a las risas y deleites, llantos y lloros y pasiones mortales los
siguen; finalmente, a mucho descanso y sosiego, mucho pesar y
tristeza. (VIII, 137)

[We see our fairest days, our clearest sunshines, are overcast with
clouds, darkness and rain: our solaces and delights are swallowed
up by dolours and by death; laughter, mirth and merriments are
waited on by tears, lamentations and other the like mortal
passions. In a word ... (for) much ease and much quietness, much
pain and much heaviness.]

This consciousness of mortality among the characters
implies a consciousness of their own mortality, although
more often they seem to be aware of the mortal danger faced
by the others. It is surprising that the egotistical Calisto
seems to refer to his own mortality more than the others,
although this is usually expressed in terms of courtly-love
imagery from the *cancioneros* and in conceits and word-play
about life and death in the loved one. This is a conscious
authorial irony, as for example when Calisto sings a song by
Diego de Quiñones: 'En gran peligro me veo / En mi muerte

no hay tardanza' (VIII, 139). [In peril great I live, / And straight of force must die.] Calisto usually expresses his impatience in mortal terms, as when in Act V he awaits the arrival of Pármeno and says: 'Agora tengo por cierto que es más penoso al delincuente esperar la cruda y capital sentencia, que el acto de la ya sabida muerte' (105) ['Now I verily believe that more painful to a felon is the expecting of that his cruel and capital sentence, than the act itself of his certain and fore-known death'], or in Act VI when he awaits the news about Melibea and says to Celestina: 'Madre mía, o abrevia tu razón o toma esta espada y mátame' (107) [Good mother, either cut off thy discourse, or take thou this sword and kill me]; and later 'Si no quieres, reina y señora mía, que desespere y vaya mi ánima a perpetua pena' . . . (108). [If thou wilt not, thou that art sole queen and sovereign of my life, that I die desperate, and that my soul go condemned from hence to perpetual pain.] For Calisto, Melibea is an angel of death and he remarks on 'áquel gesto angélico y matador' (108) [that angelical face, whose frowns murder . . .]. Her power to kill is reiterated when Calisto reacts to Celestina's catalogue of the signs of love in Melibea: '¿Y a ésas llamas señales de salud? Pues ¿cuáles serán mortales? No por cierto la misma muerte . . .' (108). [Be these . . . signs of health? What then are those that are mortal? Why, death itself could not be half so deadly.] Celestina also has a fatal power over the oblivious Calisto: 'Agora doy por bienempleada mi muerte, puesta en tales manos' (112). [Therefore do I hold my death happily employed, since that I have put it into such hands.] Calisto even compares his dreams of Melibea to Socrates' and Alcibiades' premonitory dreams, and he fears the same fatal outcome: 'pero en vida o en muerte, alegre me sería vestir su vestidura' (114). [Though I for my part, be it alive or dead, would any way be glad to see myself clothed with anything that is hers.] Despite these

obvious premonitions, Calisto nevertheless asks God to bring
him death: 'Rogaré a Dios que aderece a Celestina y ponga
en corazón a Melibea sin remedio o dé fin en breve a mis
tristes días' (VIII, 140). [I will pray (to God) that He will
direct Celestina, and put my remedy into Melibea's heart, or
else that he will shorten my sorrowful days.] Again, after his
servants' death, he says: 'Pluguiera a Dios que fuera yo ellos y
perdiera la vida y no la honra' (XIII, 187). [Would I had
(been) them and had lost my life, so I had not lost my
honour.]

The other characters have fewer premonitions of their
deaths, but as usual Pármeno is most aware of his danger,
while Sempronio is fearful at any suggestion of death, as
when he exclaims to Celestina:

¿Qué dices de sirvientes? Parece por tu razón que nos puede venir a
nosotros daño de este negocio y quemarnos con las centellas que
resultan de este fuego de Calisto. ¡Al diablo daría yo sus amores!
(III, 79)

[What sayest thou of servants? Thinkest thou that any danger is
like to come unto us, by labouring in this business? or that we shall
be burned with those sparkles which scatteringly fly forth of
Calisto's fire?]

Like Calisto, Pármeno plays with the courtly concept of
love/death in Act VII, when he says of Areúsa: 'Que me ha
muerto de amores su vista' (131) [for she hath wounded me
to death]. Celestina compares Areúsa to the seductive (and
lethal) siren of mythology in this act. In Act XI, Rojas
foreshadows death in a *Tragicomedia* interpolation, when
Pármeno compares Melibea to the siren and then adds:
'purgará su inocencia con la honra de Calisto y con nuestra
muerte' (166). [She . . . will . . . purge her innocency with
Calisto's honour and our deaths.] But in Act XII Pármeno's
realization of his danger and imminent death culminates
with an aside: '¡sacarte han el alma, sin saber quién!' (170)

[Thy (soul) shall be taken from thee . . . and thou not know who was he that did it], and again, 'Esperáramos aquí la muerte con nuestro amo, no siendo más de él merecedor de ella' (171). [We stayed here, expecting together with our master no less than death, though we did not so much deserve it as he did.] Symbolically, Sempronio and Pármeno try to flee death when a noise frightens them: 'Huigamos la muerte, que somos mozos' (175) [let us shun death; for we are both young]. When they discover that it was nothing, Pármeno claims: 'Tragada tenía ya la muerte' (176) [Death had e'en almost swallowed me up (lit.: I had already swallowed Death)], and in effect Act XII ends when Sempronio and Pármeno throw themselves out of Celestina's window.

Celestina and Melibea are interdependent in their premonitions of death. Celestina fears death when she visits Melibea's house for the first time: 'Si con el hurto soy tomada, nunca de muerta o encorozada falto, a bien librar' (IV, 86). [If the theft be found about me, I shall be either killed, or carted with a paper crown set upon my head.] For her part Melibea says that she is going to drop dead at the sound of Calisto's name; in effect she does eventually fall to her death. Celestina mentions risking her life in Calisto's service on several occasions: '¿Con qué pagarás la vieja que hoy ha puesto su vida al tablero por tu servicio? . . . Mi vida diera por menor precio, que agora daría este manto raído y viejo' (VI, 106). [How canst thou make this old woman amends, who hath hazarded her life in thy service? . . . I would have given my life for less than the price of this old tattered mantle.] But despite these premonitions, in the banquet scene Celestina resigns herself to decay and death of old age: 'Cerca ando de mi fin. En esto veo que me queda poca vida . . . envejecí para morirme' (IX, 150). [By this I know that I am near to my end, and that the lease of my life is now expiring . . . (I) grow old to die.] Melibea has no such illusions; she identifies Celestina as the instrument of her destruction in Act x, and sees death variously as a result of impatience ('¡Oh, cómo me muero con tu dilatar!' 157) [Oh how thou killest me with delays!] or death as a result of Celestina's prescribed cure for her malady ('¡Oh, por Dios, que me matas!', 158) [O (God), you kill me!]. Celestina calls the cause of Melibea's fatal illness, love, 'una blanda muerte' (159) [a gentle death]. After the first night of love with Calisto, Melibea has a clear premonition of her death when she fears the bloody reaction of her mother were she to find out about her loss of virginity: '¡Como serías cruel verdugo de tu propia sangre! ¡Cómo sería yo fin quejosa de tus días!' (XIV, 192) [How cruel a butcher wouldst thou become of thine own blood! And how doleful an end should I be of thy days!].

As for the characters' premonitions of the deaths of others, Calisto is the favourite subject since virtually everyone predicts a fatal end to his affair. In contrast, the oblivious Calisto seems less aware of the risks run by his associates. Although Celestina is worried about her own fate, only Elicia shares this worry with her. Again, Pármeno is the most prudent character, although in the final analysis he pays no attention to his own warnings. His premonitions of Calisto's death appear in Act II with the well-known lines:

Señor, porque perderse el otro día el neblí fue causa de tu entrada en la huerta de Melibea a le buscar; la entrada causa de la ver y hablar; la habla engendró amor; el amor parió tu pena; la pena causará perder tu cuerpo y el alma y hacienda; y lo que más de ello siento es venir a manos de aquella trotaconventos, después de tres veces emplumada. (77)

[Then thus, sir, your losing of your hawk the other day was the cause of your entering into the garden where Melibea was to look if she were there; your entering, the cause that you both saw her and talked with her; your talk engendered love; your love brought forth

your pain; and your pain will be the cause that you will destroy
your body, soul and goods. And that which grieves me most is that
you must fall into the hands of that same trot-up-and-down that ...
hath been three several times implumed.]

He also contrasts his own hard words with Sempronio's
blandishments:

que lo ceban, atizan tu fuego, avivan tu amor, encienden tu llama,
añaden astillas que tenga que gastar hasta ponerte en la sepultura.
(78)

[which feed your humour, quicken your love, kindle afresh your
flames, and join brands to brands, which shall never leave burning,
till they have quite consumed you and brought you to your grave].

Celestina also is aware that Calisto is doomed; when she
visits Melibea she calls him 'un enfermo a la muerte' (IV, 94)
[one whom I left sick to the death] and compares his music to
Hadrian's, 'las que compuso ... de la partida del ánima, por
sufrir sin desmayo la ya vecina muerte' (99) [those (songs)
which that great emperor and musician Hadrian composed
concerning the soul's departure from the body, the better to
endure without dismayment his approaching death]. When
Celestina tells Calisto of her success at her first interview with
Melibea, this inspires more forebodings in Pármeno: 'no es
mucha su vida; luto habremos de medrar de estos amores'
(VI, 107) [Sure, he cannot live long . . . every man his
mourning weed, and there's an end], and even Sempronio
responds to Calisto's amorous excesses with: 'Que mucho
hablando matas a ti y a los que te oyen. Y así perderás la vida
o el seso' (115). [By talking and babbling so much as you do,
you kill both yourself, and those which hear you; and so by
consequence, overthrow both thy life and understanding.]
Later he says of Calisto's impatience: 'Si tú pides que se
concluya en un día lo que en un año sería harto, no es mucha
tu vida' (VIII, 140). [If you will have that concluded in a day,

which it will if it be effected in a year, your life cannot be long.] When Calisto attends church to make sacrilegious entreaties, Pármeno exclaims, with infernal symbolism: 'Allá fue a la maldición, echando fuego . . .' (xix, 146). [He flung from us (to hell) with a vengeance . . . sparkling forth fire.] Pármeno's last lucid moment occurs in Act xii when he says of Calisto: 'soy cierto que esta doncella ha de ser para él cebo de anzuelo o carne de buitrera' (170). [For I am assured that this damsel is but the bait to this hook . . . or that flesh which is thrown out to vultures.] Even Melibea has her premonitions in Act xiv: she is frightened that something might have happened to Calisto on the way to her garden, and when he appears she warns him: 'no saltes de tan alto, que me moriré en verlo' (190) [leap not down so high, you kill me, if you do], a double premonition of both their deaths.

Melibea's death and her parents' downfall are also fore-shadowed. Sempronio says: 'Melibea es única a ellos; faltándoles ella, fáltales todo el bien' (III, 84). [Melibea is the one child to them both, and she miscarrying miscarried with her all their happiness.] Melibea foresees the possible destruction of her parents in Act iv: '¿Perder y destruir la casa y honra de mi padre por ganar la de una vieja maldita como tú?' (96). [Wouldst thou have me overthrow and ruin my father's house and hour, for to raise that of such an old rotten bawd as thou art?] And Lucrecia notes that Melibea's fate is sealed in Act x: 'ya no tiene tu merced otro medio, sino morir o amar' (161). [Your ladyship hath no other remedy . . . but either to die or to (love).] As for the other characters, Elicia is afraid that Celestina will fall to her death, as Gilman has noted:[3] 'tropezarás donde caigas y mueras' (xi, 167) [for you may hap to stumble, where you may so fall that it may be your death]. And even Calisto has a premonition of the future when he compares Celestina to Adeleta the Tuscan: 'La cual tres días ante de su fin pronunció la muerte de su viejo marido y de dos hijos que tenía' (vi, 112) [who three days before she died divined of the death of her husband and two sons]. But Calisto is so foolish that his premonition is funny.

As for imprecations and exclamations, they are full of irony, for example Pármeno's '¡allá irás con el diablo!' in Act ii, 78 [the devil go with thee]. Even Melibea threatens Celestina with 'Pues yo te certifico que las albricias que de aquí saques, no sean sino estorbarte de más ofender a Dios, dando fin a tus días' (iv, 96). [But I assure thee, the reward that thou shalt get thereby, shall be no other, save that I may take from thee all occasion of farther offending heaven, to give an end to thy evil days.] In Act vi Sempronio threatens Pármeno, first with Calisto's anger and then with sickness: '¡Oh intolerable pestilencia y mortal te consuma, rijoso . . .!' (108). [Let some intolerable mortal disease or some pestilent plague . . . consume thee, thou quarrelsome . . . caitiff!] The threat of disease is used against Sempronio in Act ix when Elicia says: '¡De mala cancre sea comida esa boca desgraciada, enojosa!' (146). [Now the evil canker eat and consume that unpleasing and offensive mouth of thine!] Lucrecia's asides against Celestina in the same act are violent: '¡Así te arrastren, traidora!' (153) [would thou wert as well dragged along the streets, thou old traitorous hag!.] The characters even invoke their own deaths, for example Calisto's 'Muerto soy de aquí allá' (xi, 165). [I die till that hour come]. Finally, the deaths in Act xii are orchestrated with imprecations: Sempronio's '¡Pues guárdese del diablo, que sobre el partir no le saquemos el alma!' (xi, 167) [But let (her) beware the devil and heed that we (not take her soul) when we come to divide the spoil!], and again his 'No mando un maravedí aunque caiga muerto' (xii, 180) [if my life lay on it, I know not where to have one farthing]; and finally, Celestina's '¡A osadas que me maten, si no te has asido una palabrilla que te dije el otro día . . .!' (xii, 180). [Now I think upon it, let me be hanged or die any other death, if thou hast not took hold of a little word, that carelessly slipped out of my mouth the other day . . .]

In the additional acts of the *Tragicomedia*, Rojas seems to arrange his references to death with even more care and attention, for example Pleberio's unconscious ironies spoken to Alisa in Act xvi about their own preparation for death and Melibea's preparation for marriage and life:

Alisa, amiga, el tiempo, según me parece, se nos va, como dicen, de entre las manos. Corren los días como agua de río. No hay cosa tan ligera para huir como la vida. La muerte nos sigue y rodea, de la cual somos vecinos y hacia su bandera nos acostamos, según natura. (204)

[My wife and friend Alisa, time methinks slips, as they say, from between our hands; and our days do glide away like water down a river. There is not anything that flies so swift as the life of man: death still follows us, and hedges us in on every side, whereunto we ourselves now draw nigh. We are now, according to the course of nature, to be shortly under his banner.]

Later, in the second night of love in the garden (Act xix), death symbolism of the swan's song and the cypress is used intentionally in the songs and in Melibea's description of the garden:[4]

¿Por qué me dejabas echar palabras sin seso al aire, con mi ronca voz de cisne? Todo se goza este huerto con tu venida. Mira la luna cuán clara se nos muestra, mira las nubes cómo huyen. ¡Oye la corriente agua de esta fontecica, cuánto más suave murmurio y zurrío lleva por entre las frescas hierbas! Escucha los altos cipreses, cómo se dan paz unos ramos con otros por intercesión de un templadico viento que los menea. (222)

[Why didst thou suffer me to send forth my words into the air, senseless and foolish as they were, and in this hoarse swannish voice of mine? Look on the moon, and see how bright she shines upon us; look on the clouds, and see how speedily they rack away; hearken to the gurgling waters of this fountain, how sweet a murmur, and what a . . . purling they make rushing along these fresh herbs . . .; hearken to these high cypresses, how one bough makes peace with another by the interecession of a . . . temperate wind, which moves them to and fro.]

Dean W. McPheeters has already studied what he calls 'the element of fatality' in these acts, and concludes that there is a consistent treatment of fatalism in Rojas' addition and interpolations.

Calisto scales Melibea's wall with Tristán and Sosia in attendance; he
falls to his death.

7

Is Melibea a tragic figure?

With the figure of Melibea, the medieval Christian reader of (or listener to) *Celestina* is presented with a genuine dilemma. Unlike Calisto, Melibea does not seem to be a parodic figure, although she too has her roots in the traditions of courtly love. As we have seen, she is an informed reader of *Cárcel de Amor*. But she is also a psychologically convincing portrait of a young woman who falls madly in love to the point of perdition. She resists Calisto's advances vehemently in the first act, but subsequently falls under the spell of Celestina and Calisto. Although Melibea's love for Calisto may be explained by her character, Celestina's magic spell may indeed be an effective one; P. E. Russell has shown convincingly that the spell cast by Celestina comes straight from contemporary witchcraft practices.[1] Celestina draws a magic circle and pours oil over a skein of thread while performing her enchantments. She takes this thread to Melibea's house where she sells it to the girl and in return extracts a piece of Melibea's clothing, her girdle, under the pretence that it will help cure Calisto of a toothache, a typical lover's malady.[2] Celestina has worked a *philocaptio* enchantment, capturing the will of the love object, and the skein is its instrument. The item of the victim's clothing completes the enchantment. Thus Melibea's will may be imprisoned by Celestina, which effectively removes her from blame for her sin in a Christian sense. Although some didacticists insist that Melibea should have been more wary, in fact Celestina appealed to her Christian charity with the story about Calisto's toothache.[3] Melibea seems the only real candidate for status as a tragic figure in *Celestina* since she is caught in a chain of events outside her control and her only flaw has been her pity. This is not dissimilar to the love-potion device in the Tristan story, and Melibea's passionate character once the spell has worked rather suggests Isolde.

The dilemma is clear. The medieval Christian was required by church doctrine to believe the witchcraft motif, which effectively makes Melibea an innocent victim. The more sophisticated, modern reader can find equal textual support for the view that Melibea was infatuated by Calisto all along, as she seems to confess in Act x to Celestina (although it might be argued that she could still be under the influence of witchcraft in this as well). Alisa's careless behaviour might equally be explained away by her stupidity and forgetfulness, plus coincidence (the opportune illness of a relative). However, although a modern Christian can deliver a moralistic verdict against Melibea, a medieval Christian could not. And if Rojas is indeed condemning his heroine for her lack of moral fibre, he must do so from the vantage point of his sceptical *converso* background, a background which took a dismissive view of witchcraft,[4] rather than from an orthodox Christian point of view. This is one more example of Rojas' ambivalence towards his characters and his message.

If Calisto's favourite reading may be supposed to be fifteenth-century Spanish songbooks – as we have seen, he sings a song from them – Melibea's literary formation had been more serious. Although she has read sentimental romances, according to her own report her father Pleberio has given her not those romances which have turned the head of her lover Calisto like some fifteenth-century Don Quixote, but rather 'those ancient books' as she calls them, full of the aphorisms and exempla of classical authors, a number of which she cites shortly before her suicide. However, some of these books handed from father to daughter seem not to have been very ancient: for example, Boccaccio's *Fiammetta*, in the Spanish translation[5] which she cites in additional Act XVI of the *Tragicomedia* when reacting to her parents' overheard plans for her future. She cites the warning given to Fiameta (the Spanish spelling), that she cannot escape love:

Passife semejablemente havía marido, y Fedra, y nos quando amamos . . . Bástete solamente hombre que de no abominable fuego, como a Mirra, a Semiramis, a Biblis, a Canace, a Cleopatra hizo, te entristeça (*Fiameta* I, 17, 44–45, 53–4; p. 105).

[Pasiphae likewise had a husband, and Phaedra, and we do when we make love ... Be satisfied that a mere man saddens you and not an abominable fire, as it did to Myrrha, Semiramis, Biblis, Canace, Cleopatra.]

Y aun otras, de mayores fuegos encendidas, cometieron nefarios e incestuosos yerros, como Mirra con su padre, Semíramis con su hijo, Cánace con su hermano y aun aquella forzada Tamar, hija del rey David. Otras aun más cruelmente traspasaron las leyes de natura, como Pasife, mujer del rey Minos, con el toro. (206)

[As likewise divers others, who were inflamed with a greater fire; and did commit most nefarious and incestuous errors, as Myrrha with her father, Semiramis with her son, Canace with her brother (as also the forced Thamar, the daughter of King David); others also in a more cruel and beastly fashion did transgress the law of nature, as Pasiphae, the wife of King Minos, with a bull.]

Interestingly, like his daughter, Pleberio also seems to have been reading this chapter recently (in Act XXI, which is Act XVI of the original *Comedia*):

Qué hizo Paris por éste, qué Elena, qué Clitemestra, qué Egisto, todo el mundo lo conoce (*Fiameta*, I, 17, ll. 24–5, p. 303).

[What Paris did for this [love], what Helen, what Clytemnestra, what Aegisthus, all the world knows.]

There is an exact echo of these words in Pleberio's:

¿Qué hizo por ti Paris? ¿qué Elena? ¿Qué hizo Hipermestra? ¿Qué Egisto? Todo el mundo lo sabe. (236)

[What service did Paris do thee? What Helena? What Clytemnestra? What Aegisthus? All the world knows how it went with them.]

The structure of his exclamations against Fortune, the world and love may also have been suggested by the structure of *Fiammetta*.

Melibea and her father seem to have got some of their ancient lore through a rather questionable source: Boccaccio's sentimental romance about a woman who is abandoned by her lover and threatens to commit suicide for the bulk of the work. *Fiammetta* colours both Melibea's choice of example and her final suicide, as critics from Castro Guisasola to Gilman have pointed out.[6] Of course both Melibea and Pleberio rely heavily on Petrarch for their list of examples as well, Melibea on *De remediis* I, 52 in Act XX, Pleberio on *Epistolae familiares* 12 and 2 in Act XXI.[7] Petrarch's Latin works may more convincingly be called 'libros antiguos', but are still not the works of classical authors which may be inferred from Melibea's words.

Melibea also reveals a knowledge of popular songs and ballads in Act XVI when she overhears her parents discussing the possibility of marrying her off. Like Calisto, she also models herself on previous literature, but she sees herself as the heroine of a ballad or the popular lyric of the unhappily married beauty, the 'bella malmaridada', when she says:

Si pasar quisiere la mar, con él iré, si rodear el mundo, lléveme consigo, si venderme en tierra de enemigos, no rehuiré su querer . . . que más vale ser buena amiga que mala casada. (206)

[If he will go to sea, I will go with him; if he will round the world I will along with him; if he will sell me for a slave in the enemy's country, I will not resist his desires . . . for it is better to be well beloved than ill married.]

Melibea seems to be thinking of the well-known:

> La bella malmaridada
> de las más lindas que vi,
> si habéis de tomar amores,
> vida, no dejéis a mí.

> [Unhappily married girl,
> the most beautiful I have seen,
> if you will take a lover
> my life, don't forget me.]

Margit Frenk says of this song, 'su fama misma era proverbial'[8] [even its fame was proverbial]. Perhaps Melibea also knew the *endecha* 'Señor Gómez Arias', whose second stanza reads:/'Señor Gómez Arias / vos me trajistes / y en tierra de moros / vos me vendistes'. [Señor Gomez Arias /you took me away / and in Moorish lands / you sold me.] Besides this verbal coincidence, *Celestina* contains another echo of this *endecha*:

> Si mi triste madre
> tal cosa supiese,
> con sus mesmas manos
> la muerte se diese.

> [If my sad mother
> were to know such a thing
> with her own hands
> she would kill herself.]

After losing her virginity in Act XIV, Melibea exclaims 'Oh pecadora de ti, mi madre, si del tal cosa fueses sabidora, cómo tomarías de grado tu muerte y me la darías a mí por fuerza' (192). [O my poor mother, if thou didst but know what we have done, with what willingness wouldst thou take thine own death! And with what violence and enforcement give me mine!]

In Act XVI Melibea rebels against her parents and contrasts herself with women of the Bible and of classical antiquity, citing her Boccaccian list of monsters of nature and incest like Canacea, Myrrha, Semiramis, Thamar. On the verge of suicide she again contrasts herself with a Petrarchan catalogue of killers like Prusias, Ptolemy, Orestes, Nero, Medea. Why did Rojas, in these *Tragicomedia* additions and interpolations, have Melibea compare herself, even negatively, to such monsters?[9] Calisto makes the more expected comparison:

Si hoy fuera viva Elena, por quien tanta muerte hobo de griegos y troyanos, o la hermosa Pulicena, todas obedecerían a esta señora por quien yo peno (117)

[If Helen were now alive, for whom so great a slaughter was made of Greeks and Trojans, or fair Polixena, both of them would have done their reverence to this lady, for whom I languish],

but even this comparison with Helen of the romance of Troy makes reference to slaughter. Melibea, a young girl who sees herself as an exotic rebel from the popular lyric, in the imagery used by herself and the other characters is a monster of nature who will contribute to the death of her lover, and perhaps to that of her mother, and who will commit suicide. In *Celestina*'s world of dialogic discourse Melibea's posturing as a literary heroine soon leads from the rôle of rebel to the rôle of killer. 'Yo cubrí de luto y jergas en este día casi la mayor parte de la ciudadana caballería' (229) [I, even this very day, have clothed the greater part of the Knights and gentlemen of this city in mourning], she says, and she is right (although she is perhaps not as culpable as she believes). The lady of court poetry whose looks kill becomes a real basilisk.

Pármeno compares her to the siren, and further adds, 'soy cierto que esta doncella ha de ser para él cebo de anzuelo o carne de buitrera' (170). [For I am assured that this damsel is but the bait to this hook . . . or that flesh which is thrown out to vultures, whereof he that eateth, is sure to pay soundly for it.]

Again, Rojas' attitude towards his possibly tragic heroine seems deeply ambivalent. Metaphorically she is both victim and predator, both blameless child and monstrous murderer of her old parents. Theologically, she must be condemned for the mortal sin of suicide, whether or not she is a victim. Unlike Calisto and Celestina she does not cry out for confession at her death, and there is therefore no possibility of redemption *in articulo mortis*.[10] She believes that she will be reunited with Calisto in hell.

From the point of view of classical tragedy, Melibea may be a somewhat more straightforward tragic heroine. She is caught in a web of events outside her own making and over which she has little control. Pluto and the three Fates (i.e. the devil) invoked by Celestina have robbed her of the will to see clearly what she is doing when she arranges a second meeting with Celestina; she reinterprets her initial encounter with Calisto as love at first sight. Her own view of herself in Act XVI is passive: she was captivated by Calisto and entreated by the astute Celestina, over several visits.

Her lament and suicide give her the pathetic stature of a Dido. But she chooses not Dido but Medea to compare herself with: a doubly inept comparison, since rather than kill herself Medea killed her children and abandoned the abandoner. Melibea may be harking back to the independence of spirit declared in Act XVI, but the reality is different, despite her brave words that she does not wish to dirty the knots of matrimony nor to follow in the marital footsteps of another man, nor does she want a father or other relative.

'Faltándome Calisto, me falte la vida' (207) [for in losing my Calisto, I lose my life], she concludes in a notable piece of dramatic foreshadowing. Reality is not the brave independence of a Medea, but the trapped and sequestered position of a post-adolescent girl in her father's home whose future prospects are either marriage or the cloister. With Calisto's death she can no longer hope to run away with him to the Moorish lands of popular song, which in any case were always a pipe-dream. Calisto's death cuts off her fantasy escape route; Melibea is trapped in the tomb of Pleberio's house, garden and tower. She can only follow her lover to death and, she hopes, to hell, like Dante's Paolo and Francesca, who are never mentioned but may be implicit in the text. From a totally anachronistic feminist point of view, the modern reader may indeed see Melibea as a tragic heroine, since her social position is undoubtedly that of victim and her only way of making an effective social protest is by her suicide. But Rojas himself seems to take a much more ambivalent attitude towards his heroine, perhaps a masculine point of view which cannot psychologically accept the idea of woman as an innocent victim and must also project her as temptress, siren, and vulture bait.

This is not to suggest that Rojas is hard on Melibea and soft on Calisto. As we have seen, Calisto is presented in most of the work as a parodic boor, with intentions which, in the *Comedia* at least, seem strictly dishonourable. Only a Melibea, blinded by love, could persist in calling him, as she does twice, a 'dechado de cortesía' [paragon of courtliness], although her readings of sentimental romance could also have coloured her perceptions. Significantly she quotes *Cárcel de Amor* to her father before she dies ('cuando el corazón está embargado de pasión, están cerrados los oídos al consejo' (229) [when the heart is surcharged with sorrow, the ear is deaf to good counsel]), and eschews quoting to him from the ancient books which he has given her. She seems almost too eager to accept responsibility for Calisto's death. 'Yo cubrí de luto y jergas en este día casi la mayor parte de la ciudadana caballería' (229). [I, even this very day, have clothed the greater part of the Knights and gentlemen of this city in mourning.] Significantly, Melibea implicates Fortune and the Fates in his death: 'Cortaron las hadas sus hilos' (230) [Thus did the destinies cut off his thread], reinforcing the undercurrent of classical tragedy. As the desire to join him after death is Dantesque, so the reading of sentimental romance influences her request to be buried beside Calisto. But the death which Melibea inflicts on the entire company is not the death of a Leriano who allows himself to pine away from unrequited love of Laureola. It is a more brutal death of the picaresque world which Rojas creates around his lovers, who have their heads turned by the reading of sentimental romances.

Melibea hurls herself from the tower while Pleberio and Alisa look on.

8

Pleberio's lament, *Cárcel de Amor*, and the *Corbacho*

Alfonso Martínez de Toledo's *Corbacho* and Diego de San Pedro's *Cárcel de Amor* are the Spanish vernacular texts which have contributed the most to *Celestina*, and it is not surprising to discover that they, as well as the Petrarchan sources, are prominent in the genesis of Pleberio's lament. Rojas undoubtedly took the 'Llanto de su madre de Leriano' as the prose model for his lament, although the *planctus* is a sturdy rhetorical tradition from ancient times and there is no shortage of models. The *planctus* was an important division of rhetoric with its own rules; it was a *digressio* from the *laus* or *enkomion*, itself a subdivision of the *apostrophe*. Certain rhetoric and imagery were obligatory: *exclamatio* and *interrogatio*, light and darkness imagery, the world-upside-down topic, the exclamation against death.[1] Furthermore, most laments seem to have at least some of the ingredients of grief as it is clinically described in the twentieth century: shock and searching, anger and guilt, bargaining, grief itself, and acceptance.[2]

In *Cárcel*, Leriano's mother begins with the praise of her son:

¡ tú en edad para bevir; tú temoroso de Dios; tú amador de la virtud; tú enemigo del vicio; tú amigo de amigos; tú amado de los tuyos! (173)

[You, of an age to live; you, a God-fearing man; you, a lover of virtue; you, an enemy of vice; you, a friend of friends; you, beloved by all your servants and vassals.][3]

Anger and guilt follow; Leriano's mother exclaims against death:

¡O muerte, cruel enemiga, que ni perdonas los culpados ni asuelves los inocentes! Tan traidora eres, que nadie para contigo tiene defensa; amenazas para la vejez y lievas en la mocedad; a unos matas por malicia y a otros por enbidia; aunque tardas, nunca olvidas; sin ley y sin orden te riges. (173)

[Oh, death, cruel enemy, who neither pardons the guilty nor spare the innocent! You are so treacherous that no one has any defence against you. You make your threats against old age, and carry off those in the flower of their youth. Some you slay out of malice and others because of envy. You may arrive late, but you never forget to come. You observe no rule or reason.]

San Pedro introduces the world-upside-down topic. Why did death reverse the natural order and let the mother die before the son?

Más razón havía para que conservases los veinte años del hijo moço que para que dexases los sesenta de la vieja madre. ¿Por qué bolviste el derecho al revés? Yo estava harta de ser biva y él en edad de bevir. (173–4)[4]

[There was greater cause for you to spare the twenty years of the youthful son than to pardon the sixty years of the aged mother. Why did you turn the natural order of things upside down? I was tired of living, and he was of an age to live.]

Bargaining with death follows:

Perdóname porque assí te trato, que no eres mala del todo, porque si con tus obras causas los dolores, con ellas mismas los consuelas levando a quien dexas con quien levas; lo que si conmigo hazes, mucho te seré obligada; en la muerte de Leriano no hay esperança, y mi tormento con la mía recebirá consuelo. (174)[5]

[Forgive me that I abuse you so, for you are not wholly evil, for if by your actions you cause grief, with those same actions you give comfort when you carry off those you have left behind to join those you hav̇ e already taken. And if you take me I shall be deeply in your debt. When Leriano dies I shall have nothing left to live for, and with my own death my torment will be eased.]

Next come grief and depression itself; the mother has survived only to grieve:

¡O hijo mío! ¿qué será de mi vejez contenplando en el fin de tu joventud? Si yo bivo mucho, será porque podrán más mis pecados que la razón que tengo para no bivir. ¿Con qué puedo recebir pena más cruel que con larga vida? Tan poderoso fue tu mal que no tuviste para con él ningund remedio; ni te valió la fuerça del cuerpo, ni la virtud del coraçón, ni el esfuerço del ánimo; todas las cosas de que te podías valer te fallecieron. (174)

[Oh my son! What sort of old age can I have when I consider how your youth was ended? If I live much longer it will be because my sins weigh heavier than my reasons for ceasing to live. What greater punishment could be inflicted upon me than long life? Your malady was so powerful that you could find no remedy for it: the strength of your body could not assist you, nor the goodness of your heart nor the valour of your spirit. All the things to which you might have had recourse failed you.]

Finally we reach acceptance:

si por precio de amor tu vida se pudiera conprar, más poder tuviera mi deseo que fuerça la muerte; mas para librarte della, ni tu fortuna quiso, ni yo triste, pude; con dolor será mi bevir y mi comer y mi pensar y mi dormir, hasta que su fuerça y mi deseo me lieven a tu sepoltura. (174).

[If your life could be bought for the price of love, my love would prove more powerful than death. But your fate would not consent to your deliverance, and I alas, could do nothing. In sorrow shall I eat and drink and think and sleep until death's power and my desire carry me to join you in the tomb.]

Pleberio's lament, like the lament of Leriano's mother, also begins with shock: '¡Ay, ay, noble mujer! Nuestro gozo en el pozo. Nuestro bien todo es perdido. ¡No queramos más vivir!' (232). [Ay me, my most noble wife! Our solace is in the suds . . . all our happiness is quite overthrown; let us now no longer desire to live.] He searches for friends to accompany his grief: '¡Oh gentes que venís a mi dolor!'. '¡Oh amigos y señores, ayudadme a sentir mi pena!' (232). [O ye good people, who come to behold my sorrows, and you gentlemen, my loving friends, do you also assist to bewail my misery!] *Exclamatio* and *interrogatio* are chief features of this style:

Oh duro corazón de padre, ¿cómo no te quiebras de dolor, que ya quedas sin tu amada heredera? ¿Para quién edifiqué torres; para quién adquirí honras; para quién planté árboles; para quién fabriqué navíos? ¡Oh tierra dura! ¿cómo me sostienes? ¿Adónde hallará abrigo mi desconsolada vejez? (232)

[O the hard heart of a father, why does thou not burst forth with grief . . . to see thyself bereaved of thy beloved heir? For whom didst thou build these turrets? For whom got I honours? For whom planted trees? For whom built ships? O hard-hearted earth, why dost thou bear me any longer? Where shall my disconsolate old age find any resting place?]

He then begins his series of angry exclamations against Fortune, the world and love. Bargaining appears with the world-upside-down topos:

Oh fortuna variable, ministra y mayordoma de los temporales bienes, ¿por qué no ejecutaste tu cruel ira, tus mudables ondas, en aquello que a ti es sujeto? ¿Por qué no destruiste mi patrimonio; por qué no quemaste mi morada; por qué no asolaste mis grandes heredamientos? Dejárasme aquella florida planta, en quien tú poder no tenías; diérasme, fortuna flutuosa, triste la mocedad con vejez alegre; no pervertieras la orden. Mejor sufriera persecuciones de tus engaños en la recia y robusta edad, que no en la flaca postrimería. (232–3)

[O variable fortune . . . thou ministress and high stewardess of all temporal happiness, why didst thou not execute thy cruel anger upon me? Why didst thou not overwhelm him with thy mutable waves, who professes himself to be thy subject? Why didst thou not rob me of my patrimony? Why didst thou not set fire on my house? Why didst thou not lay waste mine inheritance so as thou hadst left me that flourishing young plant, over which you oughtest not to have had such power? Thou mightest, o fortune, fluctuant and fluent as thou art, have given me a sorrowful youth and mirthful age, neither have therein perverted order. Better could I have borne thy blow, better endured thy persecutions, in thy my more strong and oaky age than in this my weak and feeble declining.]

Guilt is suggested in his exclamation against the world; he kept his part of the bargain but the world failed to keep hers:

¡Oh vida de congojas llena, de miserias acompañada; oh mundo, mundo! Muchos mucho de ti dijeron, muchos en tus cualidades metieron la mano, a diversas cosas por oídas te compararon; yo por triste experiencia lo contaré, como a quien las ventas y compras de tu engañosa feria no prósperamente sucedieron, como aquel que mucho ha hasta agora callado tus falsas propiedades, por no encender con odio tu ira, porque no me secases sin tiempo esta flor que este día echaste de tu poder (233)

[O life fulfilled with grief and accompanied with nought but misery! O world, world! Much have men spoken of thee, much have men writ concerning thy deceits and much have I heard myself: and mine own woeful experience is able to say something of thee as one who have been in the unfortunate fair, and have often bought and sold with thee, but never had anything that succeeded happily with me. As one who many a time heretofore, even to this present hour, have silenced thy false properties, and all because I would not purchase thy displeasure, and pull thy hatred upon me and that thou shouldst not untimely pluck this flower from me, which this day thou hast cropped by the mightiness of thy power.]

This mercantile imagery appears in *Cárcel* as well: 'si por precio de amor tu vida se pudiera comprar, más poder tuviera mi deseo que fuerça la muerte' (174). [If your life could be bought for the price of love, my love would prove more powerful than death.] Rojas later reverses this notion of payment; love pays its followers with death: 'no sólo de cristianos, mas de gentiles y judíos y todo en pago de buenos servicios' (236) [not only of Christians but of Gentiles and of Jews and all forsooth in requital of their good services].

The Petrarchan passage of contradictory images then appears, followed by a chain of baiting and trapping images perhaps suggested by Manrique's *Coplas*.[6] Courtly love provides the next imagery:

Muchos te dejaron con temor de tu arrebatado dejar; bienaventurados se llamarán, cuando vean el galardón que a este triste viejo has dado en pago de tan largo servicio. (233)

[Many have forsaken thee, fearing thy sudden forsaking of them and may well they style themselves happy, when they shall see how well thou hast rewarded this poor heavy sorrowful old man for his long service.]

This is followed by the old saw 'Quiébrasnos el ojo y úntasnos con consuelos el caxco' (233).[7] [Thou dost put out our eyes, and then to make us amends thou anointest the place with oil.]

Grief takes over fully when Pleberio fails to find any story from antiquity and Petrarch to console him in his bereavement:

Agora perderé contigo, mi desdichada hija, los miedos y temores que cada día me espavorecían: sola tu muerte es la que a mí me hace seguro de sospecha. ¿Qué haré, cuando entre en tu cámara y retraimiento y la halle sola? ¿Qué haré de que no me respondas, si te llamo? ¿Quién me podrá cubrir la gran falta que tú me haces? Ninguno perdió lo que yo el día de hoy, aunque algo conforme parecía la fuerte animosidad de Lambas de Auria, duque de los atenienses, que a su hijo herido con sus brazos desde la nao echó en la mar. Porque todas éstas son muertes que, si roban la vida, es forzado de cumplir con la fama. (34–5)

[Now shall I lose together with thee, most unhappy daughter, those fears, which were daily wont to affright me. Only thy death is that which makes me secure of all suspicions and jealousies. What shall I do, when I shall come into thy chamber and thy withdrawing room, and shall find it solitary and empty? What shall I do, whereas I shall call thee, and thou shalt not answer me? Who is he that can supply that want which thou hast caused? Who can stop up that great breach in my heart which thou hast made? Never any man did lose that which I have lost this day, though in some sort that great fortitude of Lambas de Auria, Duke of Genoa, seemeth of suit . . . who seeing his son was wounded to death, took him and threw him with his own arm forth of the ship into the sea. But such kind of deaths as these, though they take away life, yet they give reputation.]

Instead of ending the lament in a mood of acceptance, Rojas places there his bitterest words, an accusation of love. Guilt also reappears in this passage:

Herida fue de ti mi juventud, por medio de tus brasas pasé. ¿Cómo me soltaste, para me dar la paga de la huida en mi vejez? Bien pensé que de tus lazos me había librado, cuando los cuarenta años toqué, cuando fui contento con mi conyugal compañera, cuando me vi con el fruto que me cortaste el día de hoy. No pensé que tomabas en los hijos la venganza de los padres. (235)

[I was wounded by thee in my youth: I did pass through the midst of thy flames. Why didst thou let me scape? Was it that thou might'st pay me home for my flying from thee then, in mine old age? I had well thought that I had been freed from thy snares, when I once began to grow towards forty; and when I rested contented with my wedding consort, and when I saw I had that fruit, which this day thou hast cut down; I did not dream that thou wouldst in the children have taken vengeance of the parents.]

Some specific echoes of *Cárcel* appear in this passage:

Enemigo de amigos, amigo de enemigos, ¿por qué te riges sin orden ni concierto? (*Cel.*, 235–6)

[Thou art an enemy to thy friends and a friend to thy enemies; and all this because thou dost not govern thyself according to order and reason.]

A unos matas por malicia, y a otros por enbidia; aunque tardas, nunca olvidas; sin ley y sin orden te riges. (*Cárcel*, 173)

[Some you slay out of malice and others because of envy. You may arrive late, but you never forget to come. You observe no rule or reason.]
The beatitudes are glossed by both authors:

Bienaventurados los que no conociste o de los que no te curaste. Dios te llamaron otros, no sé con qué error de su sentido traídos. Cata que Dios mata los que crió; tú matas los que te siguen. (*Cel.*, 235)

[Happy are they who have not known thee, knowing thee have not cared for thee. Some, led with I know not what error, have not sticked to call thee a god . . . God does but kill those whom he hath created, and thou killest those that do follow thee.]

Bienaventurados los baxos de condición y rudos de engenio, que no pueden sentir las cosas sino en el grado que las entienden, y malaventurados los que con sotil juizio las trascenden, los cuales con el entendimiento agudo tienen el sentimiento delgado. (*Cárcel*, 173)

[Blessed are the base of nature and the rude of wit, for they feel things only in the degree to which they understand them; and unhappy are those of subtle judgement who comprehend all, those who because of acute understanding have delicacy of feeling.]

There is also some borrowing from the Archpriest of Talavera's *Corbacho*. The exemplum of Fortune and Poverty which appears in the fourth part of the *Corbacho* supplies material for Pleberio's exclamation against the world:

¡Guay de los desaventurados que a ti esperan nin esperança en ti tienen, que de todo lo que dizes dígote que non tienes nada! ¡O cuitada, non te conosçes con tu orgullo, vanagloria e pompa, e engannas todo el mundo! Mandas mucho e das poco; prometes a montones e dasles mucha nada; convidas con esperança e dasles mala andança. ¡O engannadora inica e traidora, falsa e baratera! (*Corbacho*, 279)

[Woe to the unfortunate who await you or have any hope in you: as for all you say, I tell you, you have nothing! O wretch, you know yourself not with your pride, vainglory and pomp, and you deceive all the world. You promise much and give little; you promise mountains and give a lot of nothing; you invite with hope and give them a bad time. O iniquitous and treacherous deceiver, false and cheapjack!]

This is echoed in *Celestina*'s 'Prometes mucho, nada no cumples; échasnos de ti, porque no te podamos pedir que mantengas tus vanos prometimientos' (233). [Thou promisest mountains, but performest mole-hills; and then thou dost cast us off, that we may not put thee in mind of making good thy vain promises.] Also compare the *Corbacho*'s 'Fablar mucho e prometer farto, poco dar e mucho rallar: esto sé que ay en ti' (284) [talk a lot and promise a lot, give little and rail on: I know that this is all there is to you]. *Celestina*'s

¿Cómo me mandas quedar en ti, conociendo tus falsías, tus lazos, tus cadenas y redes, con que pescas nuestras flacas voluntades? (235)

[How wouldst thou have me to rely upon thee, I knowing thy falsehoods, thy gins, thy snares, and thy nets, wherein thou entrap'st and takest our weak and feeble wills?]

reflects the *Corbacho*'s

'¿Non fui yo sabia de me apartar de todas estas cosas e inconvinientes e lazos del falso mundo, e quererme allegar a esta pobreza que tengo, e ser pobre como soy yo, non curando de tu mundo, nin de tus negocios e baratos, nin de tus imaginaçiones e pensamientos; perdiendo comer e bever e dormir los que te creen . . .?' (283)

[Was I not wise to take myself away from all these problems and snares of the false world, and to wish to arrive at my present poverty, and to be poor as I am, not worrying about your world, nor your dealings and bargains, nor your imagination and thoughts, those who believe you losing appetites and thirst and sleep . . .?]

Despite the fact that he is reasoning clearly in this passage, Pleberio returns to incoherent exclamations at the end of the lament:

Del mundo me quejo, porque en sí me crié, porque no me dando vida, no engendrara en él a Melibea; no nacida, no amara; no amando, cesara mi quejosa y desconsolada postrimería. (236)

[I complain me of the world, because I was bred up in it; for had not the world given me life, I had not therein begot Melibea; not being begot, she had not been born; not being born, I had not loved her; and not loving her, I should not have mourned, as now I do, in this my latter and uncomfortable old age!]

is followed by the incoherent

¡Oh mi compañera buena, y oh mi hija despedazada! ¿Por qué no quisiste que estorbase tu muerte? ¿Por qué no hobiste lástima de tu querida y amada madre? ¿Por qué te mostraste tan cruel con tu viejo padre? ¿Por qué me dejaste, cuando yo te había de dejar? ¿Por qué me dejaste penado? ¿Por qué me dejaste triste y solo in hac lachrymarum valle?

[O my good companion! O my bruised daughter, bruised even all to pieces! Why wouldst thou not suffer me to divert thy death? Why wouldst thou not take pity of thy kind and loving mother? Why didst thou show thyself so cruel against thy aged father? (Why hast thou left me when I should have left you?) Why hast thou left me thus in sorrow? Why hast thou left me comfortless, and all alone, *in hac lachrimarum valle*, in this vale of tears and shadow of death?]

I find Peter Dunn's suggestion, that the 'hac lachrymarum valle' at the end is a hopeful reference to the *Salve
regina*, an unlikely solution.[8] Rather, instead of reaching a
state of acceptance, Pleberio seems to regress at the end of the
lament into shock, incoherence and anger. Although the
traditional form of the lament and Rojas' model Diego de
San Pedro would suggest that acceptance should be the final
note of a *planctus*, Rojas is a writer who often employs a
commonplace to destroy a commonplace.

Pleberio's voice also fulfils the requirements of novelistic
discourse: his lament is an ironic reworking of the 'llanto de
la madre de Leriano' from *Cárcel de Amor*, which makes a
bitter comment on the failure of Petrarchan neo-stoicism to
function for Pleberio in his moment of crisis and agony. Just
as the Petrarchan examples which he lists fail to have any
relevance to his situation, just as the remedies against both
fortunes, good and bad, fail to have any significance in the
face of disaster, so the lament fails in its primary function. It
does not lead to acceptance and resignation but to the
desolation or isolation of the survivor who is sad and alone in
this vale of tears. As Shipley expresses it most eloquently:

Shattered finally, along with memory and the bodies of loved ones,
is confidence in the therapeutic and prophylactic function of
exampla and *sententiae*. We know now, we can see from the terminal
perspective of Act XXI, that Rojas' schematic characterization of
that fourth sort of reader (Those who affirm the usefulness of
authorized truth – 'colige la suma para su provecho' – and trust
memory to store, retrieve, and reapply truth with the efficiency we
now admire in the well-programmed computer) is caustic and
sardonic.[9]

9

Conclusion: Rojas' ambivalence towards literature

What, can we conclude, was Rojas' attitude towards literature? All of the literary models fail at the end of the work:
courtly love, classical antiquity, neo-stoicism, scholastic
lore, aphorisms, even estates satire. But all the characters are
using these models to serve their appetites. Celestina's
aphorisms are used to pervert morality. Calisto's courtly
posturing serves his lust. Melibea tries to justify her actions
with classical examples. Pármeno and Sempronio disguise
their self-interest behind student lore. Areúsa and Elicia hide
behind the Archpriest of Talavera's satiric and parodic
models, but at least they survive to tell the tale. Pleberio's
neo-stoical posturing is exposed as a sham when he is visited
with a genuine catastrophe.

To analyse the failure of literary models more closely,
Melibea tries to justify her actions with classical examples,
using a 'worst-case' analysis of her actions. In Act xvi she
introduces a list of classical monsters of adultery, incest and
bestiality – Venus, Myrrha, Semiramis, Canacea, Thamar,
Pasiphae – to excuse her fornication. In Act xx she looks at
murderers – Prusias, Ptolemy, Orestes, Nero, Philip, Laodice, Medea, Phrates – to justify her suicide. She carefully
avoids the obvious comparison with other suicides. The
other side of the coin is an emotional definition of her activity
by popular and folkloric tyes. She will not be like the 'bella

malmaridada', but rather compares herself with the abducted 'niña de Gomez Arias' who is sold in Moorish lands and whose mother would kill herself if she knew. Reason tells Melibea that she is a monster of nature; emotion tells her that she is herself a victim. Both images are imperfect; the attempt to pattern herself on literature is a failure. In her attempt to justify her emotions through literary precedent, she resembles her father, whose neo-stoical posturings fail him. Reversing the process used by his daughter, he claims that none of his classical examples has suffered as great a loss as he, since they all had some compensations and he had none.

Another set of characters hide themselves behind aphorism to give *auctoritas* to their shabby morals. Celestina is the main perpetrator of this travesty of traditional morality, but Sempronio is not far behind her, and they both teach Pármeno their ways. Pármeno is the one character (perhaps along with Melibea) who means what he says in the first act and who means his use of *sententiae* to be taken seriously.

Three other characters are parodic and satiric. However, Calisto is unaware that his courtly posturings are a parody of courtly love; he even seems unaware that these posturings disguise his lust. Areúsa and Elicia are more aware of their literary roots; in particular Areúsa's pastiche of the travails of a maidservant is self-consciously based on the Archpriest of Talavera's *Corbacho*. The prostitutes' jealous chorus of disapproval against Melibea seems less conscious of its debt to Alfonso Martínez de Toledo, but they can be said to be his literary granddaughters rather than a parodic reaction to an existing genre. The Archpriest is the one model whom Rojas seems to respect and emulate.

Gilman in *Art* brilliantly analysed *Celestina* as a tale of human exposure to chance after the medieval world-picture had failed. I suggest further that Rojas, the archetypal medieval man of letters, the law student at a medieval university, is showing how the substitution of literary values for theological ones also fails to shield man from mutability, chance and causality, the three furies of the early Renaissance. Although Don Quixote dies, we feel that he has won a moral victory that justified his battle. But *Celestina*'s heroes are anti-heroes who fight for the main chance and for self-interest. Celestina's life may be epic in its anti-heroism, but her death is mundane and vulgar. Calisto's manner of death is banal and trivial. Only Melibea and Pleberio appeal to our sympathy: the former was unable to withstand the assault on her virtue; the latter is guilty mainly of complacency. At the end of *Celestina* even literature has failed the characters, most of whom seem to have rejected God.

The novelistic discourse of *Celestina*, what Bahktin calls the testing of the literary hero by literature itself, has led to the defeat of both hero and literature in *Celestina*. Unlike *Don Quixote*, *Celestina* has multiple heroes, or anti-heroes, where *Quixote* has only two (although the minor characters in that work are often literary types come to life). Unlike *Don Quixote's* heroes, *Celestina*'s are almost all unattractive, and when they fail there is no transcendence in their failure, and little tragedy – with the possible exceptions of Melibea and Pleberio.

Literature has been substituted for God and found wanting. Calisto is a Melibean, not a Christian, and his religion is courtly love. He is the most extreme case, but Pleberio too has substituted the philosophical writings of these neo-stoics and Petrarch for religion. Melibea derives her attitudes from her father but is not so intellectual; she compares and contrasts herself with classical and popular heroines and sex itself becomes her god. Celestina plays God, in a travesty of an earth-mother whose words are scripted by the authorities of aphoristic wisdom literature. Rojas however provides no alternatives. His distrust of the powers of rhetoric as demonstrated by Celestina's corrupting use of language suggests that his own discipline, civil law, would certainly not be held up as a viable alternative. Logic, language, and literature have all proven deceptive. However I do not believe that all of these negatives add up to a positive, or to a reaffirmation of religion. Nowhere in the text of the twenty-one acts are we told that Christianity is the alternative, and Rojas' three verses appended to the *Tragicomedia* seem too little and too late to make the case for Christianity.

In the final analysis laughter does not bring catharsis in *Celestina*, although it can make life tolerable. The *converso* Rojas lampoons the conventions of a hostile society whose hypocrisies must be paid lip-service. Perhaps this, then, is the final tragedy of the work. Life parodies literature but both laughter and literature fail in the end. Pleberio alone is left to rant against the world, the flesh – and fortune. The devil, in the person of Celestina, is already dead, fittingly, perhaps, since God has also been carelessly discarded along the way, at least by the characters, if not by the author as well, who has performed the neatest disappearing trick in world literature.

Notes

1. Introduction: Celestina *and novelistic discourse*

1 See Stephen Gilman's introduction to my Alianza edition of *La Celestina* (Madrid, 1969 etc.).
2 *The Dialogic Imagination: Four Essays by M. M. Bakhtin*, ed. Michael Holquist, trans. Caryl Emerson and Michael Holquist (Austin: University of Texas Press, 1981, repr. 1983 etc.).
3 José Luis Canet Vallés has suggested to me that Sempronio and Pármeno are both more and less than parodies; that their pseudo-student knowledge reflects the reality of medieval university life, when servants acquired a smattering of their student master's knowledge through exposure to lectures and exposure to their master's dialectic.
4 See Dean W. McPheeters' 'La "dulce ymaginación" de Calisto', in *Estudios humanísticos sobre 'La Celestina'* (Potomac, Maryland: Scripta Humanistica, 1985), 62–70.
5 I disagreed with this analysis in *Memory in 'La Celestina'* (London: Támesis, 1970), and still feel that in the *Comedia* Areúsa only pretends to be shy and Elicia doesn't realize the extent of her dependence on Celestina. Once Celestina is gone Elicia is unable to function on her own and Areúsa, whose sense of self in the banquet scene was fierce, can try to take Celestina's place.
6 Jerry R. Rank, 'Narrativity and *La Celestina*', in *Hispanic Studies in Honor of Alan D. Deyermond: a North American Tribute*, ed. John S. Miletich (Madison: Hispanic Seminary of Medieval Studies, 1986), 235–46.
7 Oxford: Clarendon Press, 1982; paperback, 1985.
8 *The Halfway-House of Fiction: Don Quixote and Arthurian Romance* (Oxford: Clarendon Press, 1984).
9 Reprinted as Marcelino Menéndez y Pelayo, *La Celestina*, Colección Austral, 691 (Madrid: Espasa Calpe, 1947).
10 Buenos Aires: EUDEBA, 1962.
11 *A Literary History of Spain: The Middle Ages* (London: Ernest Benn, 1971), 169–70.

12 *Celestina: Tragicomedia de Calisto y Melibea*, Illinois Medieval Monographs, I, 2 vols. Champaign: University of Illinois Press, 1985). Authorship is discussed throughout volume I.

13 '*Celestina*: the Marciales Edition', *BHS*, LXIV (1987), 237–43.

2. The prefatory material: the author's ambivalent intentions

1 See P. E. Russell, 'The Art of Fernando de Rojas', *BHS*, XXXIV (1957), 160–7 (review article on Stephen Gilman's *The Art of 'La Celestina'* [Madison: University of Wisconsin Press, 1956, repr. New Jersey: Greenwood Press, 1976; trans. as '*La Celestina': arte y estructura*, Madrid: Taurus, 1974]).

2 Irony as we know it is of course a modern definition of the term; see D. C. Muecke's discussion of the issue in *Irony*, The Critical Idiom, XIII (London: Methuen, 1970). Cándido Ayllón classifies the various types of irony in *Celestina* as anticipatory, dramatic, and verbal in 'La ironía en *La Celestina*', *RF*, XXXII (1970), 37–55. Additions to the debate have been made by Jack Himelblau, 'A Further Contribution to the Ironic Vision in the *Tragicomedia*', *RoN*, IX (1967–8), 310–13; Joseph Szertics, 'Notas sobre un caso de ironía en *La Celestina*', *RoN*, XI (1969-70), 629–32; Katherine K. Phillips, 'Ironic Foreshadowing in *La Celestina*', *KRQ*, XXI (1974), 469–82; and Cándido Ayllón, *La perspectiva irónica de Fernando de Rojas* (Madrid: Porrúa Turanzas, 1984).

3 See María Rosa Lida de Malkiel's *La originalidad artística de 'La Celestina'*. She studies genre, theatrical technique and characters, devoting sub-categories to classical antecedents in each case.

4 The parody of the courtly lover has been studied by June Hall Martin, *Love's Fools: Aucassin, Troilus, Calisto, and the Parody of the Courtly Lover* (London: Támesis, 1972), 71–134. A seminal article in the growth of this argument was Alan Deyermond's 'The Text-Book Mishandled: Andreas Capellanus and the Opening Scene of *La Celestina*', *Neophil.*, XLV (1961), 218–21.

5 In quoting the text, I use my own edition of *La Celestina* (Madrid: Alianza, 1969, etc.). The translations are from James Mabbe's 1631 edition of *The Spanish Bawd* corrected against his ca. 1598 manuscript version. If there is no Mabbe version I supply my own translations. The Mabbe quotations are from my dual-text edition of *La Celestina* (Warminster: Aris and Phillips, 1987). Also see Guadalupe Martínez Lacalle, *Celestine or the Tragick-Comedie of Calisto and Melibea, translated by James Mabbe* (London: Támesis, 1972).

6 I quote from Paul Nixon, tr., *Plautus*, I, LCL (London: Heinemann, 1916, etc.), 10ff. Lida de Malkiel gives a summary of the genre debate in *Originalidad*, 29–78, and points out the dramatic nature of the work. To the original category of dialogue novel more recent critics have added morality play (Marcel Bataillon, '*La Célestine' selon Fernando de Rojas*, Paris: Didier, 1961) and 'pure dialogue' (Gilman, *Art*).

7 See *Observaciones sobre las fuentes literarias de 'La Celestina'*, *RFE* Suppl. v (1924, repr. 1973), 51ff. Castro Guisasola doubts that Rojas knew the *Amphitryon* directly, but since Rojas' contemporary Erasmus was familiar with it I doubt that it was being kept a secret from the University of Salamanca at that time.

8 Rojas wrote the *argumentos* to the additional acts in the *Tragicomedia* and possibly the *argumento* to the whole work (or this might have beeen the work of the primitive author); the editors supplied *argumentos* for the individual sixteen acts of the *Comedia*. See Stephen Gilman, *Art*, 212–16. Rojas writes a new *argumento* for Act xiv of the *Tragicomedia*.

9 See Colbert Nepaulsingh, 'The Rhetorical Structures of the Prologues of the *Libro de buen amor* and *La Celestina*', *BHS*, li (1974), 325–34.

10 Ed. José F. Montesinos, Clás. Cast. 86 (Madrid: 'La Lectura', 1928; repr. Madrid: Espasa-Calpe, 1976 etc.), 182.

11 For the former category see Gilman's *Art* and his *The Spain of Fernando de Rojas: the Intellectual and Social Landscape of 'La Celestina'* (Princeton: University Press, 1972, trans. as *La España de Fernando de Rojas: Panorama intelectual y social de 'La Celestina'*, Colección Persiles, 107, Madrid: Taurus, 1978). Marcel Bataillon's *'La Célestine' selon Fernando de Rojas* typifies the latter, along with the work of Otis H. Green and his disciples such as Ciriaco Morón Arroyo, whose *Sentido y forma de 'La Celestina'* (Madrid: Cátedra, 1974, 2nd edn. 1984) purports to summarize the main streams of *Celestina* criticism. Vicente Cantarino summarizes previous viewpoints and concludes that the work is moral in a generalized ethical sense; 'Didacticismo y moralidad de *La Celestina*', in *'La Celestina' y su contorno social: actas del I Congreso Internacional sobre 'La Celestina'*, ed. Manuel Criado de Val (Barcelona: HISPAM/Borrás, 1977), 103–9.

12 Gilman, *The Spain*, 51–64.

3. Genre and the parody of courtly love

1 *Love's Fools*, 71–134.

2 'Cervantes: a Question of Genre', in *Mediaeval and Renaissance Studies on Spain and Portugal in Honour of P. E. Russell* (Oxford: Society for the Study of Mediaeval Languages and Literature, 1981), 69–85. Northrop Frye, *The Secular Scripture: a Study of the Structure of Romance* (Cambridge, Mass: Harvard UP, 1976). For a recent opinion that *Celestina* is neither novel nor play, see Ian Michael, 'Epic to Romance to Novel: Problems of Genre Identification', *Bulletin of the John Rylands University Library of Manchester*, LXVIII (1986), 498–527, at pp. 520–3.

3 *Literary History*, 169–70.

4 Marcelino Menéndez y Pelayo's long chapter on 'La Celestina' in *Orígenes de la novela* articulated this view at length. It was questioned extensively by Inez MacDonald, 'Some Observations on the *Celestina*', *HR*, XXII (1954), 264–81, who identified Calisto as a victim of love

madness. J. M. Aguirre developed this argument in his *Calisto y Melibea, amantes cortesanos* (Zaragoza: Almenara, 1962). June Hall Martin's *Love's Fools* embodies the first lengthy analysis of the parodic nature of Calisto. Also see Nicholas G. Round, 'Conduct and Values in *La Celestina*', in *Mediaeval and Renaissance Studies on Spain and Portugal in Honour of P. E. Russell*, 38–52. Further minor contributions to this discussion have been made by John Devlin, '*La Celestina*', a Parody of *Courtly Love: toward a Realistic Interpretation of the 'Tragicomedia de Calisto y Melibea*' (N. Y.: Anaya–Las Américas, 1971), and by Gay Abbate, 'The *Celestina* as a Parody of Courtly Love', *Ariel*, III (1974), 29–32.

5 John Jones, *On Aristotle and Greek Tragedy* (London: Chatto & Windus, 1962, 2nd edn. 1968), 56. In an article on 'Aristotle's *Ethics* and *La Celestina*' in *La Corónica*, X (1981–2), 54–8, I have suggested that Aristotle's categories of virtues and vices may have influenced Rojas' portrayal of the characters.

6 In Diego de San Pedro, *Obras completas*, II, ed. Keith Whinnom (Madrid: Castalia, 1971), translated by Whinnom as *Prison of Love, 1492, together with the Continuation of Nicolás Núñez, 1496* (Edinburgh: Edinburgh UP, 1979).

7 Gilman, *The Spain*, 329–30. The original index is found in Fernando del Valle Lersundi, 'Testamento de Fernando de Rojas, autor de *La Celestina*', *RFE*, XVI (1929), 366–88.

8 Quoted in Castro Guisasola, *Observaciones*, 129.

9 *Carta al Profesor Stephen Gilman sobre problemas rojanos y celestinescos a propósito del libro 'The Spain of Fernando de Rojas'* (Mérida, Venezuela: Facultad de Humanidades, University of the Andes, 1973, 2nd edn 1975, 1983), 75; repeated in *Celestina: Tragicomedia de Calisto y Melibea*, I, Act IV. 83, p. 93.

10 D. P. Walker, *Spiritual and Demonic Magic from Ficino to Campanella*, Studies of the Warburg Institute, 22 (London: Warburg Institute, 1958), especially 3–24.

11 *Libro de música de vihuela de mano intitulado El Maestro*; the picture is reproduced in David Munrow, *Instruments of the Middle Ages and Renaissance* (London: Oxford University Press, 1976), 84.

12 Walker, *Magic*, 12–24.

13 'Antipater quidem Sidonius tam exercitati ingenii fuisse creditur, ut versus hexametros aliosque diuersorum generum ex improuiso copiose diceret', *Rerum memorandarum* 2, 2, 20 (Quoted in Castro Guisasola, *Observaciones*, 128).

14 See Alan Deyermond, 'The Worm and the Partridge: Reflections on the Poetry of Florencia Pinar', *Mester*, VII (1978), 3–8.

15 Deyermond stresses their disgust at Calisto's lack of control in '*Hilado – Cordón – Cadena*: Symbolic Equivalence in *La Celestina*', *Ce.*, I, i (May, 1977), 6–12.

16 'Lyric Traditions in Non-Lyrical Genres', in *Studies in Honor of Lloyd*

A. Kasten (Madison: Hispanic Seminary of Medieval Studies, 1975), 39–52.

17 Second edn, Madrid: Cátedra, 1977, no. 222, p. 127.

18 *Antología de albas, alboradas y poemas afines en la Península Ibérica hasta 1625* (Madrid: Playor, 1976), 81, 123, 132. Also see her comments on *Celestina* in '*Albor': Mediaeval and Renaissance Dawn-Songs in the Iberian Peninsula* (London: King's College, 1980), especially 33, 41, 63.

19 See E. M. Wilson and S. M. Stern's study of the Spanish tradition in *Eos: an Enquiry into the Theme of Lovers' Meetings and Partings at Dawn in Poetry*, ed. Arthur T. Hatto (The Hague: Mouton, 1965), 299–343. Samuel G. Armistead and James T. Monroe, '*Albas, Mammas*, and Code-Switching in the Kharjas: a Reply to Keith Whinnom', *La Corónica*, XI (1982–3), 174–207, especially 181, conclude that an *alborada* is a sign of courtship while an *alba* is a sign of an adulterous relationship.

20 On the topic of the lower classes' sexual desires for members of the upper class see Alan Deyermond, 'Divisiones socio-económicas, nexos sexuales: la sociedad de *Celestina*', *Ce.*, VIII, ii (Fall, 1984), 3–10.

21 For the debt that this passage owes to the Archpriest of Talavera, see Anthony J. Cardenas, 'The "corriente talaverana" and the *Celestina*: beyond the First Act', *Ce.*, X, ii (Fall, 1986), 31–8.

22 *The Spain*, 384–400.

23 'El ambiente concreto en *La Celestina*', in *Estudios dedicados a James Homer Herriott* (Madison: University of Wisconsin, 1966), 145–64.

4 From parody to satire: clerical and estates satire

1 'Sería candoroso interpretar el tumulto desmandado de quienes tiran sus breviarios y dejan sus rezos como rasgo "anticlerical" o como censura de *La Celestina* de liviandades eclesiásticas'. [It would be naive to interpret the untidy rabble of those who toss aside their breviaries and leave their prayers as an "anticlerical" feature or as a condemnation by *La Celestina* of clerical looseness]. Américo Castro, '*La Celestina' como contienda literaria: castos y casticismos* (Madrid: Revista de Occidente, 1965), 96–8.

2 The first translation of *Celestina*, into Italian, emphasizes the anticlericalism and mentions Franciscans and Dominicans specifically: see Kathleen V. Kish, *An Edition of the First Italian Translation of the 'Celestina' (Alfonso Hordognes, Rome, 1556)*, UNCSRLL, 128 (Chapel Hill: University of North Carolina Press, 1973), 19. At the opposite extreme, the first French translation suppresses the references and transfers them to a military sphere; see Denis L. Drysdall (ed.), *Fernando de Rojas, 'La Celestina' in the French Translation of 1578 by Jacques de Lavardin: a Critical Edition with Introduction and Notes* (London: Támesis, 1974), 21 ff.

3 These two imaginary characters reappear in Act II, when 'la moza que esperaba al ministro' is again a veiled reference to Crito by Celestina; Sempronio is duped once more. See John J. Reynolds, '"La moça que esperaua al ministro" (*La Celestina*, auto III)', *RoN*, V (1963–4), 200–2, and Denis L. Drysdall, 'Two Notes on *La Celestina*', *RoN*, XIV (1972–3), 589–92.

4 For a comprehensive study of estates satire see Jill Mann, *Chaucer and the Medieval Estates Satire: the Literature of Social Classes and the 'General Prologue' to the 'Canterbury Tales'* (Cambridge: CUP, 1973).

5 Castro, however, rejects parody as too facile a category for Rojas' art (*Contienda literaria*, 96–8). For the 'Misa de amor' theme, see Pierre Le Gentil, *La poésie lyrique espagnole et portugaise à la fin du moyen age*, 2 vols. (Rennes: Plihon, 1949, 1952), I, 194–204, II, 453–8.

6 Michael Gerli (ed.), Alfonso Martínez de Toledo, *Arcipreste de Talavera o Corbacho* (Madrid: Cátedra, 1979).

7 Deyermond, *The Petrarchan Sources of 'La Celestina'* (London: OUP, 1961; Westport, Conn.: Greenwood Press, 1975) 59.

8 Pármeno does have his tragic dimension, although it has virtually disappeared at this point. According to Russell, 'Pármeno's case seems designed to illustrate the harm that masters can do to their servants': 'Ambiguity in *La Celestina*' (review article on M. Bataillon, '*La Célestine' selon Fernando de Rojas*, *BHS*, XL, 1963, 35–40).

5. Verbal humour and the legacy of stagecraft

1 Deyermond looked at the stylistic consequences of the Petrarchan borrowings in *Petrarchan Sources*, 92–107, as did Gilman in *Art*. Gilman also investigates the uses of *sententiae* and proverbs in the first chapter of his book (37–86). George A. Shipley Jr studies a series of image clusters related to a proverb in 'El natural de la raposa: un proverbio estratégico de *La Celestina*', *NRFH*, XXIII (1974), 35–64; see also his 'Authority and Experience in *La Celestina*', *BHS*, LXII (1985), 95–111.

2 See Malcolm Read, 'The Rhetoric of Social Encounter: *La Celestina* and the Renaissance Philosophy of Language', in *The Birth and Death of Language: Spanish Literature and Linguistics (1300–1700)* (Madrid: Porrúa Turanzas, 1983), 70–96, and Leslie Turano's unpublished doctoral dissertation, 'Aristotle and the Art of Persuasion in *Celestina*' (University of London, Westfield College, 1985).

3 Several critics have commented on this passage, notably Otis H. Green, '"Lo de tu abuela con el ximio" (*La Celestina*, Auto I)', *HR*, XXIV (1956), 1–12, also Samuel G. Armistead and Joseph H. Silverman, 'Algo más sobre "Lo de tu abuela con el ximio" (*La Celestina*, I): Antonio de Torquemada y Lope de Vega', *PSA*, LXIX, 205 (1973), 11–18. A rather peculiar interpretation of the passage is offered by Alberto M. Forcadas, 'Otra solución a "lo de tu abuela con

el ximio" (Auto I de *La Celestina*)', *RoN*, xv (1974–5), 567–71, who seems to feel that the 'ximio' was Jewish. James F. Burke supplies a comprehensive summary of previous criticism and fresh insight in 'Calisto's Imagination and his Grandmother's Ape', *La Corónica*, v (1977–8), 84–90.

4 Curiously, James Mabbe's original translation of *La Celestina* amplified the obscene passages, according to Guadalupe Martínez Lacalle's edition of the original MS. The printed text suppressed these obscenities. For an analysis of the passages in question and of Mabbe's amplification of the obscenities in Act VII see Lacalle's edition of *Celestine or the Tragick-comedie of Calisto and Melibea, translated by James Mabbe*, 65f.

5 See Carmelo Samonà, *Aspetti del retoricismo nella 'Celestina'* (Rome: Facoltà di Magistero dell' Università, 1953), and Gilman, *Art*.

6 Deyermond, *Petrarchan Sources*, 59.

7 See Ramón Menéndez Pidal's discussion of this joke in 'Una nota a *La Celestina*', *RFE*, IV (1917), 50–1. A sixteenth-century *villancico* contained this expression; was it proverbial or borrowed from *Celestina*?

8 B. Bussell Thompson disagrees with Otis H. Green's interpretation of this passage as another copyist's mistake in Act I and considers it an indication of Sempronio's superficial wisdom and inadequate education; 'Misogyny and Misprint in *La Celestina*', *Ce.*, I, ii (Fall, 1977), 21–8.

9 Lida de Malkiel has studied at length all of these antecedents in *Originalidad*: Calisto, 373ff.; Melibea, 452ff.; Celestina, 537ff.; the servants, 616ff.; the girls, 676ff.; Centurio, 702ff. A valuable addition to her observations is found in the posthumous article 'Elementos técnicos del teatro romano desechados en *La Celestina*', *RPh*, XXVII (1973–4), 1–12, which goes back to ca. 1954. She points out that the comic debate between servants and comic dialogue dependent on mutual misunderstandings are missing from the work, although some of the continuations return to this tradition. See too 'La técnica dramática de *La Celestina* (texto de una conferencia inédita, leída el 21 de octubre de 1961 en la Universidad de la Plata)', in *Homenaje a Ana María Barrenechea*, ed. L. Schwartz Lerner and I. Lerner (Madrid: Castalia, 1984), 281–92. For Miguel Marciales' theories of Sanabria's authorship of acts XV, XVII and XVIII of *La Celestina* see *Celestina: Tragicomedia de Calisto y Melibea*, I, 120–94.

10 *Philosophía antigua poética*, ed. A. Carballo Picazo, 3 vols. (Madrid: CSIC, 1953), III, 24. My thanks to Paul Lewis Smith for pointing this out to me.

11 'L'Infra-Monde de la Célestinesque' in *'La Célestine' et sa descendance directe* (Bordeaux: Institut d'Etudes Ibériques et Ibéro-Américaines de l'Université, 1973), 457–538.

6. The rhetorical shift from comedy to tragedy: ironic foreshadowing and premonitions of death

1 Ironic premonition in *La Celestina* has been the subject of two articles. In 'The Element of Fatality in the *Tragicomedia de Calisto y Melibea*', *Symposium*, VIII (1954), 331–5, Dean W. McPheeters considered the additional acts, while Katharine K. Phillips, 'Ironic Foreshadowing', discussed critical opinion and looked at some specific examples, 475–8. For irony in general see Cándido Ayllón, *La perspectiva irónica de Fernando de Rojas*.
2 Madrid: Gredos, 1963, repr. 1975.
3 Stephen Gilman treats ironic foreshadowing in the several fatal falls in *Art*, 119–32.
4 See George A. Shipley, '"Non erat hic locus": the Disconcerted Reader in Melibea's Garden', *RPh*, XXVII (1973–4), 286–303.

7. Is Melibea a tragic figure?

1 'La magia, tema integral de *La Celestina*', in *Temas de 'La Celestina' y otros estudios del 'Cid' al 'Quijote'* (Barcelona: Ariel, 1978), 241–76.
2 Geoffrey West, 'The Unseemliness of Calisto's Toothache', *Ce.*, III, i (May, 1979), 3–10.
3 Michael T. D'Emic, in his unpublished M.Litt. thesis '*La Celestina* and the Medieval Didactic Tradition' (Trinity College Dublin, 1975, 129–30) argues that *philocaptio*, according to *Malleus maleficarum*, is a strong temptation which can be resisted.
4 See Russell, 'La magia', 252–3. He concludes that the Jews were not particularly superstitious, while denying that Rojas' converso status would predispose him towards or against a belief in witchcraft.
5 Edited by Lia Mendia Vozzo, Juan Bocacio, *Libro de Fiameta*, Collana di Testi e Studi Ispanici, 4 (Pisa: Giardini, 1983).
6 Castro Guisasola, *Observaciones*, 142–5; Gilman, *Art*, VI, 3. Castro Guisasola does not spot the debt in Act XVI but does find two uses of *Fiameta* by Melibea in the first night of love, Act XIV.
7 Castro Guisasola, *Observaciones*, 126, 130–1.
8 The texts are in her *Lírica española de tipo popular*: 'La bella malmaridada', no. 293, 148; 'Señor Gómez Arias', no. 324, 158. The commentary is in *Estudios sobre lírica antigua* (Madrid: Castalia, 1978), 167–8. María Rosa Lida de Malkiel commented on the 'Gómez Arias' parallel in *Originalidad*, p. 322, n. 29, p. 424, n. 8. For Melibea's liberal upbringing by her father, see Dean W. McPheeters' 'Melibea, mujer del Renacimiento', in *Estudios humanísticos*, 7–19.
9 For Shipley Melibea's inappropriate Petrarchan catalogue at her death is symptomatic of 'the failure of reason and co-operative memory to deal adequately with her quandary' and the failure of 'foolish authority': 'Authority and Experience in *La Celestina*', 103.

10 See Anne Eesley, 'Four Instances of "¡Confesión!" in *Celestina*', *Ce*, VII, ii (Fall, 1983), 17–19, and Alan Deyermond, '"¡Muerta soy! ¡Confesión!": *Celestina y el arrepentimiento a última hora*', in *De los romances-villancicos a la poesía de Claudio Rodríguez: 22 ensayos . . . en homenaje a Gustav Siebenmann*, ed. J. M. López de Abiada and A. López Bernasocchi (Madrid: J. Esteban, 1984), 129–40.

8. Pleberio's lament, Cárcel de Amor, and the Corbacho

1 Margaret Alexiou, *The Ritual Lament in Greek Tradition* (Cambridge: CUP, 1974).
2 Colin Murray Parkes, *Bereavement: Studies in Grief in Adult Life* (Harmondsworth: Pelican, 1975; repr. Penguin, 1980).
3 The English translations are from Keith Whinnom, *Diego de San Pedro, Prison of Love, 1492, together with the Continuation of Nicolás Núñez, 1496*, 79–88. Compare this with Diego de San Pedro's lamentations of the Virgin in his *Pasión trobada* and *Siete Angustias*; for example, in both: 'el cual mi consuelo era, / el cual era mi salud; / el cual sin dolor pariera, / Él, amigas, bien pudiera / dar virtud a la virtud. / En Él tenía marido, / hijo y hermano e esposo, / de todos era querido; / nunca hombre fue nascido / ni hallado tan hermoso' (*Obras completas*, I, 156; III, 192–3). [He was my consolation / He was my health / Him I bore without pain / He could, friends, have / shown virtue to virtue. / In Him I had husband / son and brother and spouse / He was loved by all / no man born / was ever so beautiful.]
4 In the *Siete Angustias*: '¡O muerte que siempre tienes / descanso cuando destruyes! / ¡O enemiga de los bienes! / ¡a quien te fuye le vienes, / a quien te quiere le fuyes! / ¡o cruel que siempre fuiste / muy temida sin letijo! / pues ofenderme quesiste, / mataras la madre triste / dexaras vivir el fijo' (*OC*, I, 158). [O Death, you who only rest / when you destroy! / O enemy of happiness! / You come to him who flees you; / you flee him who loves you. / O cruel you were, / feared without rest! / Since you wished to harm me / you should kill the sad mother / and let the son live!] In Spain this reversal topic is found as early as *Roncesvalles*, when duke Aymón says of Reynaldos de Montalbán, 'Vos fuérades pora vivir / e yo pora morir más' [You should live / and I die instead] (ed. R. Menéndez Pidal, *Tres poetas primitivos*, 52). Exclamations against death are universal; the one in the *Libro de Buen Amor* is among the most famous: '¡Ay muerte! ¡muerta seas, muerta e malandante! / Mataste a mi vieja, ¡matasses a mí ante! /Enemiga del mundo, que non as semejante / de tu memoria amarga non es que non se espante', ed. Jacques Joset, Clás. Cast., 2 vols., 14 and 17, (Madrid: Espasa-Calpe, 1974), stanzas 1520–3. [Oh Death, be dead, dead and wretched! / You killed my old woman, rather you should kill me! / Enemy of the world, like none other, / there is no one who doesn't fear your bitter memory.]

5 Bargaining can be found in Berceo's *Duelo de la Virgen*: 'Dicía a los
  moros: 'Gentes, fe qe devedes, /matat a mí primero qe a Christo
  matedes; / si la madre matáredes, mayor merced avredes / tan buena
  creatura, por Dios, non la matedes' (ed. Arturo M. Ramoneda,
  Madrid: Castalia, 1980, st. 56). [She said to the Moors: People, behold
  / kill me before killing Christ / if you kill his mother you will have
  greater mercy; / do not kill such a good creature, for God's sake.] Juan
  de Mena uses this commonplace in the *Laberinto de Fortuna* when
  Lorenzo Dávalos' mother laments the death of her son: 'Dezía,
  llorando, con lengua raviosa: / "O matador de mi fijo cruel, / mataras
  a mí e dexaras a él, / que fuera enemiga non tan porfiosa; / fuera la
  madre muy más digna cosa / para quien mata levar menor cargo; / non
  te mostraras a él tan amargo, / nin triste dexaras a mí querellosa"' (ed.
  John G. Cummins, Madrid: Anaya, 1968, st. 205, 11. 1633–40). [She
  said, crying, with ranting voice: / Oh cruel killer of my son, / you
  should kill me and leave him; / for were you not such a stubborn
  enemy; / the mother would be a worthier thing, / so that the killer
  would not have so difficult a job; / you should not be so bitter to him /
  nor leave me in anguish.]

6 The Manrique image is in stanza 13 of the *Coplas*.

7 Cota has been suggested as the source (*Diálogo entre el Amor y un Viejo*,
  ed. Elisa Aragone, Florence: Felice Le Monnier, 1961). See H. Salvador Martínez, 'Cota y Rojas: contribución al estudio de las fuentes y la
  autoría de *La Celestina*', *HR*, XLVIII (1980), 37–55. It is, however, an old
  saw. See my 'Cota, his Imitator, and *La Celestina*: the Evidence Re-
  examined', *Ce.*, IV, i (May, 1980), 3–8.

8 *Fernando de Rojas*, TWAS, 368 (Boston: Twayne, 1975), 166.

9 'Authority and Experience', 106. While this book was at press, Luis
  Miguel Vicente published an article with a similar title, 'El lamento de
  Pleberio: contraste y parecido con dos lamentos en *Cárcel de amor*', *Ce.*,
  XII, i (May, 1988), 35–43. The approach to the material is however,
  not similar.

Bibliography

Abbate, Gay, 'The *Celestina* as a Parody of Courtly Love', *Ariel*, III (1974), 29–32

Aguirre, J. M., *Calisto y Melibea, amantes cortesanos* (Zaragoza: Almenara, 1962)

Alexiou, Margaret, *The Ritual Lament in Greek Tradition* (Cambridge: CUP, 1974)

Armistead, Samuel G. and Monroe, James T., '*Albas, Mammas, and Code-Switching in the Kharjas: a Reply to Keith Whinnom*', *La Corónica*, XI (1982–3), 174–207

Armistead, Samuel G. and Silverman, Joseph H., 'Algo más sobre "Lo de tu abuela con el ximio" (*La Celestina*, I): Antonio de Torquemada y Lope de Vega', *PSA*, LXIX, 205 (1973), 11–18

Ayllón, Cándido, 'La ironía en *La Celestina*', RF, XXXII (1970), 37–55

La perspectiva irónica de Fernando de Rojas (Madrid: Porrúa Turanzas, 1984)

Bakhtin, M. M., *The Dialogic Imagination: Four Essays*, ed. Michael Holquist, trans. Caryl Emerson and Michael Holquist (Austin: University of Texas Press, 1981, reprinted 1983 etc.)

Bataillon, Marcel, '*La Célestine' selon Fernando de Rojas* (Paris: Didier, 1961)

Berceo, Gonzalo de, *Signos que aparecerán antes del Juicio Final . . . Duelo de la Virgen*, ed. Arturo M. Ramoneda (Madrid: Castalia, 1980)

Berndt, Erna Ruth, *Amor, muerte y fortuna en 'La Celestina'* (Madrid: Gredos, 1963, repr. 1975)

Boccaccio, Giovanni, tr. as Juan Bocacio, *Libro de Fiameta*, ed. Lia

Mendia Vozzo, Collana di Testi e Studi Ispanici, 4 (Pisa: Giardini, 1983)

Burke, James F., 'Calisto's Imagination and his Grandmother's Ape', *La Corónica*, v (1977–8), 84–90

Cantarino, Vicente, 'Didacticismo y moralidad de *La Celestina*', in *'La Celestina' y su contorno social: actas del I Congreso Internacional sobre 'La Celestina'*, ed. Manuel Criado de Val (Barcelona: HISPAM/Borrás, 1977), 103–9

Cardenas, Anthony J., 'The "corriente talaverana" and the *Celestina*: beyond the First Act', *Ce.*, x, ii (Fall, 1986), 31–8

Castro, Américo, *'La Celestina' como contienda literaria: castas y casticismos* (Madrid: Revista de Occidente, 1965)

Castro Guisasola, F., *Observaciones sobre las fuentes literarias de 'La Celestina'*, *RFE* Suppl. v (1924, repr. 1973)

Cota, Rodrigo, *Diálogo entre el Amor y un Viejo*, ed. Elisa Aragone (Florence: Felice Le Monnier, 1961)

D'Emic, Michael T., *'La Celestina* and the Medieval Didactic Tradition', unpublished M. Litt. dissertation (Trinity College Dublin, 1975)

Devlin, John, *'La Celestina', a Parody of Courtly Love: toward a Realistic Interpretation of the 'Tragicomedia de Calisto y Melibea'* (N. Y.: Anaya-Las Américas, 1971)

Deyermond, Alan D., 'Divisiones socio-económicas, nexos sexuales: la sociedad de *Celestina*', *Ce.*, viii, ii (Fall, 1984), 3–10

'Hilado – Cordón – Cadena: Symbolic Equivalence in *La Celestina*', *Ce.*, i, i (May, 1977), 6–12

A Literary History of Spain: The Middle Ages (London: Ernest Benn, 1971); 2nd edn., *Historia de la literatura española: La Edad Media*, trans. Luis Alonso López (Barcelona: Ariel, 1973, etc.)

'Lyric Traditions in Non-Lyrical Genres', in *Studies in Honor of Lloyd A. Kasten* (Madison: Hispanic Seminary of Medieval Studies, 1975), 39–52

'"¡Muerta soy! ¡Confesión!": Celestina y el arrepentimiento a última hora', in *De los romances–villancicos a la poesía de Claudio Rodríguez: 22 ensayos ... en homenaje a Gustav Siebenmann*, ed. J. M.López de Abiada and A. López Bernasocchi (Madrid: J.Esteban, 1984), 129–40

The Petrarchan Sources of 'La Celestina' (London: Oxford University Press, 1961; Westport, Conn.: Greenwood Press, 1975)

'The Text-Book Mishandled: Andreas Capellanus and the Opening Scene of *'La Celestina'*, *Neophil.*, XLV (1961), 218–21

'The Worm and the Partridge: Reflections on the Poetry of Florencia Pinar', *Mester*, VII (1978), 3–8

Drysdall, Denis L. (ed.), *Fernando de Rojas, 'La Celestina' in the French Translation of 1578 by Jacques de Lavardin: A Critical Edition with Introduction and Notes* (London: Támesis, 1974)

'Two Notes on La Celestina', *RoN*, XIX (1972–3), 589–92

Dunn, Peter N., *Fernando de Rojas*, TWAS, 368 (Boston: Twayne, 1975)

Eesley, Anne, 'Four Instances of "¡Confesión!" in *Celestina*', *Ce.*, VII, ii (Fall, 1983), 17–19

Empaytaz [de Croome], Dionisia, *'Albor': Mediaeval and Renaissance Dawn-Songs in the Iberian Peninsula* (London: King's College, 1980)

Empaytaz, Dionisia, *Antología de albas, alboradas y poemas afines en la Península Ibérica hasta 1625* (Madrid: Playor, 1976)

Forcadas, Alberto M., 'Otra solución a "lo de tu abuela con el ximio" (Auto I de *La Celestina*)', *RoN*, XV (1974–5), 567–71

Fowler, Alastair, *Kinds of Literature: an Introduction to the Theory of Genres and Modes* (Oxford: Clarendon Press, 1982; paperback, 1985)

Frenk, Margit, *Estudios sobre lírica antigua* (Madrid: Castalia, 1978)

Frenk [Alatorre], Margit (ed.), *Lírica española de tipo popular*, 2nd edn (Madrid: Cátedra, 1977)

Frye, Northrop, *The Secular Scripture: a Study of the Structure of Romance* (Cambridge, Mass.: Harvard UP, 1976)

Gilman, Stephen, *The Art of 'La Celestina'* (Madison: University of Wisconsin Press, 1956, repr. New Jersey: Greenwood Press, 1976; trans. as *'La Celestina': arte y estructura*, Colección Persiles 71, Madrid: Taurus, 1974)

The Spain of Fernando de Rojas: the Intellectual and Social Landscape of 'La Celestina' (Princeton: University Press, 1972, trans. as *La España de Fernando de Rojas: Panorama intelectual y social de 'La Celestina'*, Colección Persiles, 107, Madrid: Taurus, 1978)

Green, Otis H., '"Lo de tu abuela con el ximio" (*La Celestina*, Auto I)', *HR*, XXIV (1956), 1–12

Heugas, Pierre, '*La Célestine*' *et sa descendance directe* (Bordeaux: Institut d'Etudes Ibériques et Ibéro-Américaines de l'Université, 1973)

Himelblau, Jack, 'A Further Contribution to the Ironic Vision in the *Tragicomedia*', *RoN*, IX (1967–8), 310–13

Jones, John, *On Aristotle and Greek Tragedy* (London: Chatto & Windus, 1962, 2nd edn 1968)

Kish, Kathleen V., *An Edition of the First Italian Translation of the* '*Celestina*' *(Alfonso Hordognes, Rome, 1556)*, UNCSRLL, 128 (Chapel Hill: University of North Carolina Press, 1973)

Le Gentil, Pierre, *La poésie lyrique espagnole et portugaise à la fin du moyen age*, 2 vols. (Rennes: Plihon, 1949, 1952)

Lida de Malkiel, María Rosa, 'El ambiente concreto en *La Celestina*: fragmentos de un capítulo no aprovechado para la originalidad artística de *La Celestina*', in *Estudios dedicados a James Homer Herriott* (Madison: University of Wisconsin, 1966), 145–64

'Elementos técnicos del teatro romano desechados en *La Celestina*', *RPh*, XXVII (1973–4), 1–12

'La técnica dramática de *La Celestina* (texto de una conferencia inédita, leída el 21 de octubre de 1961 en la Universidad de la Plata)' in *Homenaje a Ana María Barrenechea*, ed. L. Schwartz Lerner and I. Lerner (Madrid: Castalia, 1984), 281–92

La originalidad artística de '*La Celestina*' (Buenos Aires: EUDEBA, 1962)

López Pinciano, Alonso, *Philosophía antigua poética*, ed. A. Carballo Picazo, 3 vols. (Madrid: CSIC, 1953)

MacDonald, Inez, 'Some Observations on the *Celestina*', *HR*, XXII (1954), 264–81

McPheeters, Dean W., 'The Element of Fatality in the *Tragicomedia de Calisto y Melibea*', *Symposium*, VIII (1954), 331–5

Estudios humanísticos sobre '*La Celestina*' (Potomac, Maryland: Scripta Humanistica, 1985)

Mann, Jill, *Chaucer and the Medieval Estates Satire. The Literature of Social Classes and the* '*General Prologue*' *to the* '*Canterbury Tales*' (Cambridge: CUP, 1973)

Marciales, Miguel, *Carta al Profesor Stephen Gilman sobre problemas rojanos y celestinescos a propósito del libro 'The Spain of Fernando de Rojas'* (Mérida, Venezuela: Facultad de Humanidades, University of the Andes, 1973, 2nd edn 1975, 1983)

Martin, June Hall, *Love's Fools: Aucassin, Troilus, Calisto, and the Parody of the Courtly Lover* (London: Támesis, 1972)

Martínez, H. Salvador, 'Cota y Rojas: contribución al estudio de las fuentes y la autoría de *La Celestina*', HR, XLVIII (1980), 37–55

Martínez de Toledo, Alfonso, *Arcipreste de Talavera o Corbacho*, ed. Michael Gerli (Madrid: Cátedra, 1979)

Mena, Juan de, *Laberinto de Fortuna*, ed. John G. Cummins (Madrid: Anaya, 1968)

Menéndez y Pelayo, Marcelino, 'La Celestina', in *Orígenes de la novela* (reprinted as *La Celestina*, Colección Austral, 691, Madrid: Espasa-Calpe, 1947, etc.)

Menéndez Pidal, Ramón, 'Una nota a *La Celestina*', RFE, IV (1917), 50–1

Menéndez Pidal, Ramón (ed.), *Tres poetas primitivos*, Colección Austral, 800 (Buenos Aires: Espasa-Calpe, 1948)

Michael, Ian, 'Epic to Romance to Novel: Problems of Genre Identification', *Bulletin of the John Rylands University Library of Manchester*, LXVIII (1986), 498–527

Morón Arroyo, Ciriaco, *Sentido y forma de 'La Celestina'* (Madrid: Cátedra, 1974, 2nd edn 1984)

Muecke, D.C., *Irony*, The Critical Idiom, XIII (London: Methuen, 1970)

Munrow, David, *Instruments of the Middle Ages and Renaissance* (London: Oxford University Press, 1976)

Murray Parkes, Colin, *Bereavement: Studies in Grief in Adult Life* (Harmondsworth: Pelican, 1975; repr. Penguin, 1980)

Nepaulsingh, Colbert, 'The Rhetorical Structures of the Prologues of the *Libro de buen amor* and *La Celestina*, BHS, LI (1974), 325–34

Nixon, Paul (trans.), Plautus, *Works: Latin and English*, I, LCL (London: Heinemann, 1916, etc.)

Phillips, Katherine K., 'Ironic Foreshadowing in *La Celestina*', *KRQ*, XXI (1974), 469–82

Rank, Jerry R., 'Narrativity and *La Celestina*', in *Hispanic Studies in Honor of Alan D. Deyermond: a North American Tribute*, ed. John S. Miletich (Madison: Hispanic Seminary of Medieval Studies, 1986), 235–46

Read, Malcolm, 'The Rhetoric of Social Encounter: *La Celestina* and the Renaissance Philosophy of Language', in *The Birth and Death of Language: Spanish Literature and Linguistics (1300–1700)* (Madrid: Porrúa Turanzas, 1983), 70–96

Reynolds, John J., '"La moça que esperaua al ministro" (*La Celestina*, aucto III)', *RoN*, V (1963–4), 200–2

Riley, Edward C., 'Cervantes: a Question of Genre', in *Mediaeval and Renaissance Studies on Spain and Portugal in Honour of P. E. Russell* (Oxford: Society for the Study of Mediaeval Languages and Literature, 1981), 69–85

Rojas, Fernando de, *Celestine or the Tragick-comedie of Calisto and Melibea*, translated by James Mabbe, ed. Guadalupe Martínez Lacalle (London: Támesis, 1972)

Celestina. Edited with an introduction and notes by Dorothy Sherman Severin with the translation of James Mabbe (1631) (Warminster: Aris and Phillips, 1987)

Celestina: Tragicomedia de Calisto y Melibea. Introduction and critical edition by Miguel Marciales, edited by Brian Dutton and Joseph T. Snow. Illinois Medieval Monographs, 1, 2 vols. (Champaign: University of Illinois Press, 1985.)

La Celestina, ed. Dorothy S. Severin, intro. Stephen Gilman (Madrid: Alianza Editorial, 1969 etc.)

La Celestina, ed. and intro. Dorothy S. Severin (Madrid: Cátedra, 1987)

See also Drysdall, Kish

Round, Nicholas G., 'Conduct and Values in *La Celestina*', in *Mediaeval and Renaissance Studies on Spain and Portugal in Honour of P. E. Russell* (Oxford: Society for the Study of Mediaeval Languages and Literature, 1981), 38–52

Ruiz, Juan, *Libro de Buen Amor*, ed. Jacques Joset, Clás. Cast, 2 vols., 14 and 17 (Madrid: Espasa-Calpe, 1974)

Russell, P. E., 'Ambiguity in *La Celestina*', *BHS*, XL (1963), 35–40

'The Art of Fernando de Rojas', *BHS*, XXXIV (1957), 160–7

'La magia, tema integral de *La Celestina*', in *Temas de 'La*

Celestina' y otros estudios del 'Cid' al 'Quijote' (Barcelona: Ariel, 1978), 241–76

Samonà, Carmelo, *Aspetti del retoricismo nella 'Celestina'* (Rome: Facoltà di Magistero dell'Università, 1953)

San Pedro, Diego de, *Obras completas*, 3 vols., I, II, ed. Keith Whinnom; III, ed. Keith Whinnom and Dorothy Sherman Severin (Madrid: Castalia, 1971, 1973, 1979)

See also Whinnom

Severin, Dorothy Sherman, '*Albas* and *Alboradas* in *La Celestina'*, in *The Spirit of the Court: Selected Proceedings of the Fourth Congress of the International Courtly Literature Society, Toronto, 1983*, ed. Glyn S. Burgess and Robert A. Taylor (Cambridge: D. S. Brewer, 1985), 327–9

'Aristotle's *Ethics* and *La Celestina'*, *La Corónica*, x (1981–2), 54–8.

'Calisto and Orphic Music', in *Creation and Re-creation: Experiments in Literary Formin Early Modern Spain: Studies in Honour of Stephen Gilman* (Newark, Delaware: Juan de la Cuesta, 1983), 1–5

'*Celestina*: the Marciales Edition', *BHS*, LXIV (1987), 273–43

'Cota, his Imitator, and *La Celestina*: the Evidence Re-examined', *Ce.*, IV, i (May,1980), 3–8

'Fernando de Rojas and *Celestina*: the Author's Intention from *Comedia* to *Tragicomedia de Calisto y Melibea'*, *Ce.*, v, i (May, 1981), 1–5

'From the Lamentations of Diego de San Pedro to Pleberio's Lament', in *The Age of the Catholic Monarchs, 1474–1516: Literary Studies in Memory of Keith Whinnom*. Publications of the Bulletin of Hispanic Studies (Liverpool: University Press, 1988), 178–84

'Humour in *La Celestina'*, *Romance Philology*, XXXII (1978–9), 274–91

'Is *La Celestina* the First Modern Novel?', *Revista de Estudios Hispánicos* (Puerto Rico), IX (1982 [1984]: *Homenaje a Stephen Gilman*), 205–9

Memory in 'La Celestina' (London: Támesis, 1970)

'La parodia del amor cortés en *La Celestina'*, *Edad de Oro*, III (Madrid: Universidad Autónoma, 1984), 275–9

'Parodia y sátira en *La Celestina'*, *Actas del Sexto Congreso*

Internacional de Hispanistas (Toronto 22-26 de agosto de 1977) (Toronto: University of Toronto Press, 1980), 695-7

Shipley Jr, George A., 'Authority and Experience in *La Celestina*', *BHS*, LXII (1985), 95-111

'El natural de la raposa: un proverbio estratégico de *La Celestina*', *NRFH*, XXIII (1974), 35-64

'"Non erat hic locus": the Disconcerted Reader in Melibea's Garden': *RPh*, XXXVII (1973-4), 286-303

Szertics, Joseph, 'Notas sobre un caso de ironía en *La Celestina*', *RoN*, XI (1969-70), 629-32

Thompson, B. Bussell, 'Misogyny and Misprint in *La Celestina*, Act I', Ce., I, ii (Fall, 1977), 21-8

Turano, Leslie P., 'Aristotle and the Art of Persuasion in *Celestina*', unpublished PhD dissertation (University of London, Westfield College, 1985). Abstract in *Medieval Hispanic Research Seminar Newsletter*, I (London: Westfield College, 1985), 3

Valdés, Juan de, *Diálogo de la lengua*, Clás. Cast., 86 (ed. José F. Montesinos, Madrid: Espasa-Calpe ['La Lectura'], 1928; repr. Madrid: Espasa-Calpe, 1976 etc.)

Valle Lersundi, F. del, 'Testamento de Fernando de Rojas, autor de *La Celestina*', *RFE*, XVI (1929), 366-88

Vicente, Luis Miguel, 'El lamento de Pleberio: contraste y parecido con dos lamentos en *Cárcel de amor*', Ce., XII, i (May, 1988), 35-43

Walker, D. P., *Spiritual and Demonic Magic from Ficino to Campanella*, Studies of the Warburg Institute, 22 (London: Warburg Institute, 1958)

West, Geoffrey, 'The Unseemliness of Calisto's Toothache', Ce., III, i (May, 1979), 3-10

Whinnom, Keith (trans.), *Diego de San Pedro, Prison of Love, 1492, together with the Continuation of Nicolás Núñez, 1496.* (Edinburgh: Edinburgh UP, 1979)

Williamson, Edwin, *The Halfway-House of Fiction: Don Quixote and Arthurian Romance* (Oxford: Clarendon Press, 1984)

Wilson, E. M. and Stern, S. M., 'Iberian', in *Eos: an Enquiry into the Theme of Lovers' Meetings and Partings at Dawn in Poetry*, ed. Arthur T. Hatto (The Hague: Mouton, 1965), 299-343

Index

Castro Guisasola, F., 10, 54, 64, 77,
98, 123 n. 7, 124 n. 8, n. 13,
128 n. 6, n. 7
Celestina, 1–2, 8, 22, 27,
30–2, 38, 42–5, 50–4, 58–60,
62–80, 82–3, 85–91, 96–6, 101,
117–20, 121 n. 5, 126 n. 3,
127 n. 9
Centurio, 56, 76–7, 127 n. 9
Cervantes, 23–4, 47
Chaucer, 126 n. 4, 134
Cid, 128 ch. 7 n. 1, 136
Cide Hamete [Benengeli], 3
Claudina, 60
Cleopatra, 97
Clytemnestra (Clitemestra,
Hipermestra), 97, 98
Comedia de Calisto y Melibea, 4, 9, 10,
11, 12, 15, 19, 20, 25, 27, 59, 83,
121 n. 5
Corbacho, 53–5, 58, 105, 112–14, 118,
126 n. 6
Cota, Rodrigo, 6, 130 n. 7
Criado de Val, Manuel, 123 n. 11
Crito, 73, 77, 126 n. 3
Cummins, John G., 130 n. 5
Cupid, 46

Dante, 102, 103
Dávalos, Lorenzo, 130 n. 3
David, 97
D'Emic, Michael T., 128 ch. 7 n. 3
De causis corruptarum artium, 17
De institutione christianae feminae, 17
De remediis utriusque fortunae, 98
De triplice vita, 33
De vita coelitus, 33
Devlin, John, 124 n. 4
Deyermond, Alan, ix, 6, 24, 38, 39,
121 n. 6, n. 11, 122 n. 4, 123 n. 3,
124 n. 14, n. 15, n. 16, 125 n. 19,
126 n. 7, 126 n. 1, 127 n. 6, 129 n.
10
Diálogo de la lengua, 17
Diálogo entre el Amor y un viejo, 130 n.
7
Dido, 101
Don Quixote, 23–4, 47, 97, 119, 121
Don Quixote, 1–3, 5, 23–4, 119, 128
ch. 7, n. 1

Drysdall, Denis L., 125 n. 2, 126 n.
3
Dunn, Peter, 115, 130 n. 8

Eesley, Anne, 129 n. 10
Egisto, see Aegisthus
Elena, see Helen
Elicia, iv, viii, 38, 44, 51, 54–5, 58,
60, 73, 76–7, 83, 88, 90–1,
117–18, 121 n. 5
Eliso, 77–8
el Maestro, 33, 124 n. 11
Empaytaz [de Croome], Dionisia,
40, 125 n. 18, 133
Epicurean, 83
Epistolae familiares, 32, 98
Erasmus, 123

Fates, 101, 103
Fedra, see Phaedra
Fernandus Servatus, 10
Fiammetta (Fiameta), 97, 98
Fiammeta (Fiameta), 97, 128 n. 5,
n. 6
Ficino, Marsilio, 33–4, 124 n. 10
Forcadas, Alberto M., 126 ch. 5 n. 3
Fortune, 103, 108–9, 112
Fowler, Alastair, Kinds of Literature,
4–5, 121 n. 7
Francesca, 102
Frenk [Alatorre], Margit, 40, 99,
128 n. 8; Lírca española de tipo
popular, 40, 125 n. 17, 128 n. 8
Frye, Northrop, 24, 123 n. 2

Genette, 4
Genoa, 111
Gerli, Michael, 126 n. 6, 135
Gilman, Stephen, ix, 4, 47, 60, 69,
90, 98, 121 n. 1, 122 n. 1, 123 n.
8, n. 11, n. 12, 124 n. 7, n. 9, 125
n. 22; The Art of 'La Celestina', 4,
58, 118, 122 n. 1, n. 6, 123 n. 8,
n. 11, 126 n. 1, 127 n. 5, 128 ch. 6
n. 3, 128 n. 6
Gómez Arias, 99, 117, 128 n. 8
Green, Otis H., 123 n. 11, 126 ch. 5
n. 3, 127 n. 8
Guevara, Antonio de, 17

Hadrian (Adriano), 32, 89
Hatto, Arthur T., 125 n. 19
Hector (Héctor), 31
Helen (Elena), 97–8, 100
Herriott, James Homer, 125 n. 23
Heugas, Pierre, 80, 127 n. 11
Himelblau, Jack, 122 n. 2
Hipermestra, see Clytemnestra
Hordognes, Alfonso, (Ordóñez,
  Alfonso), 125 n. 2

Isolde, 96

Jerusalem (Jerusalén), 71
Jones, John, 124 n. 5
Joset, Jacques, 129 n. 4
Julius Caesar, 80

Kasten, Lloyd A., 124–5 n. 16
Kish, Kathleen V., 125 n. 2

Lambas de Auria, 110
Laodice, 117
Laureola, 29, 103
Lavardin, Jacques de, 125 n. 2
Lazarillo, 4
Lazarillo, 2–3
Le Gentil, Pierre, 126 n. 5
Leriano, 1, 26–9, 103, 105–7;
  Leriano's mother, 105–8
Lerner, I., 127 n. 9
Lerner, L. Schwartz, 127 n. 9
Lewis Smith, Paul, 127 n. 10
Libro de Buen Amor, 123 n. 9, 129 n. 4
Lida de Malkiel, María Rosa, 4, 122
  n. 3, n. 6, 125 n. 23, 127 n. 9, 128
  n. 8; La originalidad artística de 'La
  Celestina', 5–6, 48, 121 n. 10, 122
  n. 3, n. 6, 127 n. 9, 128 n. 8
Lope de Vega, 126 ch. 5 n. 3
López Bernasocchi, A., 129 n. 10
López de Abiada, J. M., 129 n. 10
López Pinciano, Alonso, 80, 127 n.
  10
Lucenda, 1
Lucrecia, iv, viii, 22, 37, 42, 57,
  74–6, 90–1

Mabbe, James, 122 n. 5, 127 n. 4
MacDonald, Inez, 123 n. 4

McPheeters, Dean W., 93, 121 n. 4,
  128 ch. 6 n. 1, 128 n. 8
Macedonia, 29
Malleus maleficarum, 128 ch. 7 n. 3
Mann, Jill, 126 n. 4
Manrique, Jorge, Coplas por la muerte
  de su padre, 110, 130 n. 6
Marciales, Miguel, 124 n. 9; Celestina
  edition, 6, 32, 122 n. 12, n. 13,
  124 n. 9, 127 n. 9
Martin, June Hall, 23, 70, 122 n. 4,
  123 n. 1, 124 n. 4; Love's Fools, 70,
  122 n. 4, 123 n. 1, 124 n. 4
Martínez, H. Salvador, 130 n. 7
Martínez de Toledo, Alfonso,
  Archpriest of Talavera, 4, 53–5,
  58, 105, 112, 117–18, 125 n. 21,
  126 n. 6
Martínez Lacalle, Guadalupe, 122
  n. 5, 127 n. 4
Martorell, 5
Medea, 100, 101–2, 117
Melibea, 1–2, 4, 22, 24–7, 29–32,
  35–9, 41–7, 54–5, 58, 63–4, 69–71,
  73–6, 85–92, 94; (a tragic figure?)
  95–103; 104, 114, 117–18, 124 n.
  4, 127 n. 9, 128 ch. 6 n. 4, 128 n.
  6, n. 8, n. 9
Mena, Juan de, Laberinto de Fortuna,
  130 n. 5
Mendia Vozzo, Lia, 128 n. 5
Menéndez y Pelayo, Marcelino, 'La
  Celestina' in Orígenes de la novela, 5,
  121 n. 9, 123 n. 4
Menéndez Pidal, Ramón, 127 n. 7,
  129 n. 4
Mercury, 10
Michael, Ian, 123 n. 2
Milán, Luis de, 33
Miletich, John S., 121 n. 6
Minerva, 72
Minos, 97
Monroe, James T., 125 n. 19
Montesinos, José F., 123 n. 10
Morón Arroyo, Ciriaco, 123
  n. 11
Muecke, D. C., 122 n. 2
Munrow, David, 124 n. 11
Murray Parkes, Colin, 129 n. 2
Myrrha (Mirra), 97, 100, 117

CAMBRIDGE IBERIAN AND LATIN AMERICAN STUDIES

A list of books in the series will be found at the end of the volume.

HISTORY AND SOCIAL THEORY

ROBERT I. BURNS: *Muslims, Christians, and Jews in the Crusader Kingdom of Valencia*

MICHAEL P. COSTELOE: *Response to Revolution: Imperial Spain and the Spanish American revolutions, 1810–1840*

HEATH DILLARD: *Daughters of the Reconquest: Women in Castilian town society, 1100–1300*

ANDREW DOBSON: *An Introduction to the Politics and Philosophy of José Ortega y Gasset*

JOHN EDWARDS: *Christian Córdoba: the city and its region in the late Middle Ages*

LEONARD FOLGARAIT: *So Far From Heaven: David Aljaro Siqueiros' 'The March of Humanity' and Mexican Revolutionary Politics*

DAVID GIES: *Theatre and Politics in Nineteenth-Century Spain: Juan de Grimaldi as impresario and government agent*

JUAN LÓPEZ-MORILLAS: *The Krausist Movement and Ideological Change in Spain, 1854–1874*

MARVIN LUNENFELD: *Keepers of the City: The Corregidores of Isabella I of Castile (1474–1504)*

LINDA MARTZ: *Poverty and Welfare in Habsburg Spain: the example of Toledo*

ANTHONY PAGDEN: *The Fall of Natural Man: the American Indian and the origins of comparative ethnology*

EVELYN S. PROCTER: *Curia and Cortes in León and Castile, 1072–1295*

A. C. DE C. M. SAUNDERS: *A Social History of Black Slaves and Freedmen in Portugal, 1441–1555*

DAVID E. VASSBERG: *Land and Society in Golden Age Castile*

KENNETH B. WOLF: *Christian Martyrs in Muslim Spain*

LITERATURE AND LITERARY THEORY

STEVEN BOLDY: *The Novels of Julio Cortázar*

ANTHONY CASCARDI: *The Limits of Illusion: a critical study of Calderón*

LOUISE FOTHERGILL-PAYNE: *Seneca and 'Celestina'*

MAURICE HEMINGWAY: *Emilia Pardo Bazán: the making of a novelist*

B. W. IFE: *Reading and Fiction in Golden-Age Spain: a Platonist critique and some picaresque replies*

JOHN KING: *Sur: A study of the Argentine literary journal and its role in the development of a culture, 1931–1970*

JOHN LYON: *The Theatre of Valle-Inclán*

BERNARD McGUIRK & RICHARD CARDWELL (eds.): *Gabriel García Márquez: new readings*

JULIÁN OLIVARES: *The Love Poetry of Francisco de Quevedo: an aesthetic and existential study*

FRANCISCO RICO: *The Spanish Picaresque Novel and the Point of View*

For EU product safety concerns, contact us at Calle de José Abascal, 56–1°,
28003 Madrid, Spain or eugpsr@cambridge.org.

www.ingramcontent.com/pod-product-compliance
Ingram Content Group UK Ltd.
Pitfield, Milton Keynes, MK11 3LW, UK
UKHW012340130625
459647UK00009B/410